EXILE.

BEFORE THEM.

VOLUME

8

THE
AMERICAN HERITAGE
BOOK OF THE
PRESIDENTS
AND FAMOUS AMERICANS

★ ★ ★ ★ ★

WILLIAM McKINLEY
THEODORE ROOSEVELT
WILLIAM HOWARD TAFT

CREATED AND DESIGNED BY THE EDITORS OF
AMERICAN HERITAGE
The Magazine of History

12-VOLUME EDITION PUBLISHED BY
DELL PUBLISHING CO., INC., NEW YORK, N.Y.

William McKinley

Theodore Roosevelt

William Howard Taft

CONTENTS
OF VOLUME EIGHT

FAMOUS AMERICANS

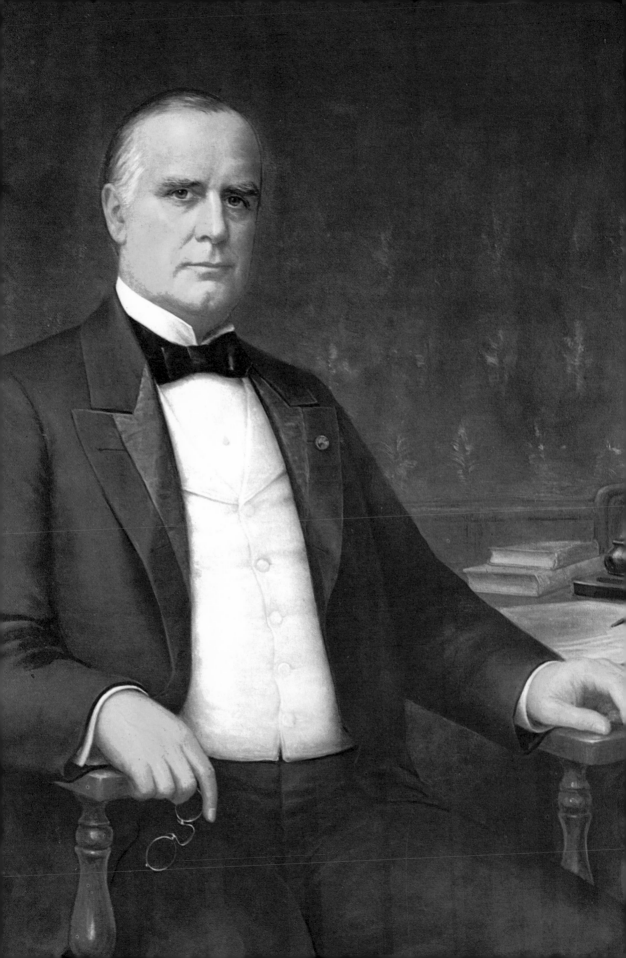

WILLIAM McKINLEY

Silent crowds watched the coffin pass through the streets of Buffalo, of Washington, and of Canton, Ohio. It was September, 1901, and the more perceptive mourners may have realized that the casket contained not only the body of an assassinated President, but the remains of an era as well. The last Civil War veteran to be elected to the White House, William McKinley had administered a war of his own, and when it was won, the American flag flew halfway around a shrinking globe. At home McKinley had seen the passing of the frontier and had bequeathed to his successor a restless people whose progress could now be measured by smoking steel mills, rising cities, and the growth of giant trusts.

But while the United States under McKinley broke with its past, it had not yet learned to read the signposts pointing to its future. On the day before he was shot, the President told visitors at the Pan-American Exposition at Buffalo: "Isolation is no longer possible or desirable. . . . The period of exclusiveness is past." And yet, despite his vision of international affairs, he did not seem to recognize the implications of the exhibition itself. He looked at the wonderful and mysterious gadgets with a childlike curiosity but without any true understanding of their portents. For the amiable McKinley was a man of the 1800's, not of the turbulent new century of which he saw so little.

William McKinley, Jr., the seventh of nine children of William and Nancy Allison McKinley, was born on January 29, 1843, in Niles, Ohio. A delicate child, he liked school and developed into a keenly observant and taciturn young man. He was religious, intelligent, and diligent, and his mother hoped that he would become a Methodist minister. At seventeen he entered Allegheny College, but had to withdraw after one term because of illness. By the time he recuperated, the family's finances were depleted and he was unable

President McKinley, by Harry T. See

to return to college. Until the outbreak of the Civil War, he taught school and clerked in a post office.

Stirred by his family's abolitionist sympathies and attracted by the excitement and glamour that war seemed to offer, McKinley enlisted in the Twenty-third Ohio Volunteer Infantry Regiment. He performed credibly through some of the bloodiest battles of the war, and his commanding officer, Rutherford B. Hayes, called him "one of the bravest and finest officers in the army."

After the war McKinley studied law for a term, was admitted to the Ohio bar, and then sought a practice in Canton, a county seat. An elderly judge accepted him as a partner and left him his practice. Friendly, handsome, self-assured, and devoid of pomposity or conceit, McKinley moved confidently in Canton's social and professional circles. A Republican, he worked on behalf of his friend Hayes when the latter ran for the Ohio governorship in 1867. McKinley established a reputation as an effective speaker and vigorous campaigner. Two years

McKinley was a handsome lad of eighteen when he enlisted in the Union army as an Ohio volunteer.

later he was nominated for prosecuting attorney of Stark County and won the post.

Clearly an up-and-coming figure in Canton, Major McKinley was the object of many a local girl's attentions. The prosecutor's own affections were centered on the socially prominent Ida Saxton, a fragile but attractive young woman who returned his love. They were married in January, 1871, and their first child, Katherine, was born on Christmas Day of that year. They were a handsome family, captivated by one another, reasonably prosperous and prominent, with a bright future before them. But just before their second child was due in the spring of 1873, Ida's mother died. The new infant, another girl, lived only a few months, and Ida sank into a mental and physical depression from which she never fully rallied. She began to have convulsions, which were accompanied by a loss of consciousness; she remained an epileptic for life and, in addition, suffered from phlebitis. Her love for Katherine might have stimulated a determination to recover, but in 1875 the four-year-old girl died. Ida was unable to reverse the decline of her mind and body. She clung possessively to her husband and insisted that he cater to her every whim. For the rest of his life McKinley bore his painful burden privately and uncomplainingly.

Politics provided the relief he needed. Elected to Congress in 1876 after a vigorous campaign, McKinley moved with his wife to a Washington hotel and struggled to pay her doctors and the bills run up by her expensive tastes. Rutherford B. Hayes was President at the time, and he introduced McKinley to the political elite. The young congressman enjoyed the masculine political world, where his cordial, graceful manner endeared him to his colleagues.

Representative McKinley was regarded as a moderate, even liberal, legislator. He favored civil service reform, Negro suffrage, the interests of the workingman; he opposed the excesses of big business. His consuming interest, however, was the tariff, and he set out to master its many intricacies. He championed protection, convinced that barriers

Republican capitalist Mark Hanna sits at the head of the table at a dinner party at his home (above). The Ohio millionaire used every means at his disposal to secure the 1896 presidential nomination for his friend McKinley (right), whose epileptic wife, Ida (center), always accompanied him to social events.

to cheap foreign goods would protect the wage scale of the American laborer and the struggling domestic industries. He considered the McKinley Tariff Act of 1890 a great achievement. Its high rates on agricultural products and manufactured goods reflected the protectionist view, although raw sugar was not taxed at all as a favor to the Sugar Trust. The act included a reciprocity arrangement that permitted the President to place duties on certain articles if he felt that nations exporting these items were imposing excessive duties on American goods.

Like most tariff legislation, the McKinley Tariff Act was controversial, but it made its author a well-known figure across the country. At the 1888 presidential nominating convention, where he endorsed the candidacy of Senator John Sherman of Ohio, McKinley refused to allow his name to be placed in nomination as a compromise candidate. But it was at this convention that Marcus A. Hanna resolved that some day McKinley would become President.

Hanna, a millionaire industrialist, was tough, shrewd, and powerful. He was called a kingmaker, but he and McKinley actually needed each other. By this time Congressman McKinley was beginning to have presidential aspirations. Hanna supplied the money and the organization while McKinley maintained his role as an idealistic statesman.

In 1890 a slump in Republican fortunes and a Democratic gerrymander in Ohio cost McKinley his seat in Congress. The next year, financed by Hanna, he ran for the Ohio governorship and was elected by a comfortable margin. The job was a routine one—the state constitution gave the governor little power—and not particularly demanding. Because he left the operation of the party machinery to Hanna, he had free time to spend with Ida, and she demanded all of it. Every day at exactly three o'clock, McKinley stepped to his office window and waved a handkerchief at his wife, who watched from their nearby home. Ida, who spent her time crocheting bedroom slippers (she reportedly made thousands of them), insisted on accompanying her husband to social affairs. He sat beside her at all functions and became adept at acting swiftly at the first sign of an epileptic attack. Quickly he would place a napkin or handkerchief over her convulsed face and retreat with her to another room. The painful scene was enacted countless times in front of embarrassed friends.

As governor, McKinley reformed the Ohio tax structure, which collected disproportionately high taxes on real estate and low taxes on corporations. He dealt with a violent coal miners' strike in 1894 by calling out the National Guard to prevent the miners from doing further damage. For the most part, however, he remained a paternalistic champion of the workingman, winning legislative approval of a board to arbitrate labor disputes and raising funds and food for strikers facing starvation.

McKinley's election to the governorship made him a front-runner for the Republican presidential nomination in 1896. But in 1893 his ability to govern the nation suddenly became questionable. An old friend, Robert Walker, had fallen victim to the financial depression and had asked McKinley to sign a seventeen-thousand-dollar note. McKinley agreed, and he continued to sign notes, thinking that the slips Walker was placing before him were renewals of the first pledge; they were, in fact, notes for additional sums. Finally Walker declared bankruptcy, and McKinley found that he had endorsed pledges totaling one hundred and thirty thousand dollars. Mark Hanna came to the rescue. He set up a trust fund and collected money from industrialists, who were reminded how much McKinley had done for business. (The donors received no favors in return for their help.) In addition, thousands of small contributions poured in from Army comrades, workingmen, and storekeepers, who regarded McKinley as an honest victim of hard times.

Later that year, McKinley was re-elected governor by a landslide. Early in 1896, he and Hanna began to prepare for his presidential quest. The depression during the Democratic administration made Republican chances seem bright, but the monetary issue so disrupted the political scene that nothing was completely predictable. McKinley tried to avoid taking a firm stand on this question, speaking out on some occasions in behalf of sound money and espousing bimetallism at other times.

Hanna, meanwhile, was more concerned about the price of delegates than the price of silver. He did not buy votes, but he awed Republican leaders with the most expensive, best-organized campaign seen up to that time. McKinley was assured of the nomination before the delegates had even convened.

Principal interest at the convention centered on what stand the party—and McKinley—would take on the money issue. The country was bitterly divided: some were for free and unlimited coinage of silver whereas others favored a gold standard exclusively. Western Republicans opposed the latter and said that espousal of it would force them out of the party. Nevertheless, McKinley and Hanna decided to declare forthrightly for gold. Their platform stated that the party was "opposed to the free coinage of silver" and that "the existing gold standard must be maintained." McKinley believed that the plank would clinch the East and give him a chance in the Midwest, where industrial workers could be told that a shift to silver would jeopardize business and their jobs. Garret A. Hobart, a New Jersey lawyer, was chosen to be McKinley's running mate.

The silverites dominated the Democratic convention in July, the high point of which was the speech by former Congressman William Jennings Bryan of Nebraska. Beginning quietly, the masterful orator built toward a peroration that thundered defiance: "Having behind us the producing masses of this nation and the world, supported by the commercial interests, the laboring interests and the toilers everywhere, we will answer their demand for a gold standard by saying to them: You shall not press down upon the brow of labor this crown of thorns, you shall not crucify mankind upon a cross of gold." The Democrats chose Bryan as their nominee, as did the prosilver Populist party.

Bryan traveled far, but had very little money to work with. McKinley, on the other hand, ran a heavily financed front-porch campaign. Hanna raised millions of dollars; he spent money lavishly on pamphlets, posters, and buttons, and gave many state delegations train fare to go and see McKinley in Canton. The railroads cooperated by offering reduced rates so that citizens from many states could journey to the home of the Republican candidate. On one day alone, McKinley spoke to some thirty thousand visitors. He won the Presidency in November by an electoral vote of 271 to 176.

One of President McKinley's first orders of business was, predictably, to restore a Republican tariff. In 1894 the Democrats had replaced the McKinley Tariff with the Wilson-Gorman Act. Having called for higher tariffs in his Inaugural Address, McKinley approved the Dingley bill of 1897, which raised rates to new highs, but empowered the President to negotiate tariff concessions with other nations.

But the tariff and other domestic issues were overshadowed during McKinley's Presidency by the prelude to, and the waging and aftermath of, the Spanish-American War. Partially because of the Wilson-Gorman Act, the Cuban sugar market collapsed in 1895, and the Cubans revolted against their Spanish overlords. Rebel leaders resolved to render the island useless to Spain: plantations and ranches were devastated under a scorched-earth policy. The Spanish governor, Valeriano Weyler, brutally herded rural families into garrisoned towns. By the end of 1897 loss of American property in Cuba amounted to sixteen million dollars.

In his Inaugural Address, McKinley had said that he wanted "no wars of conquest; we must avoid the temptation of territorial aggression." And although he was horrified by events in Cuba, he assured Carl Schurz that there would be "no jingo nonsense under my administration." The new rebellion and the destruction of United States property—along with sensational newspaper coverage that inflamed public opinion—worsened the situation, but McKinley, besieged by advice from many quarters, still preferred being called too cautious to being too rash. He gave the Spanish every opportunity to settle their differences with Cuba. The islanders, however, now wanted what Spain would not grant: full independence.

For more than a year McKinley sought a diplomatic solution. Spain refused his offers to mediate, but Governor Weyler was replaced, his policies were modified, and the Spanish ministry promised a degree of autonomy for Cuba. After the Queen Regent extended to the Antilles all rights enjoyed by Spaniards, the President told Congress

GARRET A. HOBART

Rarely had an American Vice President brought to the office ability as great as that of Garret A. Hobart. In the first two years of the McKinley administration, Senator Lodge of Massachusetts noted, Hobart "restored the Vice-Presidency to its proper position." His administrative and organizational skills were those of a brilliant lawyer, politician, and businessman. Having established a law practice in Paterson, New Jersey, in 1866, Hobart entered the state legislature in 1872, became director of several banks and corporations, and by 1895 was one of the leading Republicans in the state. Ironically, his nomination for the second spot in 1896 was due less to his superior qualities of leadership than to the Republicans' desire to carry the traditionally Democratic state of New Jersey. Elected to the Vice Presidency, Hobart presided over the Senate with intelligence and authority, working constantly to improve communications between the Upper House and the Executive. "He keeps tab on everything," remarked the Washington *Post* in admiration. An intimate of President McKinley, Vice President Hobart was, as his biographer David Magie points out, "consulted in all questions of general policy"; his prestige was so great that newspapers sometimes referred to him as the "Assistant President." Hobart died in office in November, 1899, and was mourned by President McKinley and a genuinely grieved Capital city.

that Spain should have a chance to make good its promises.

The Spanish ambassador to the United States, Dupuy de Lôme, was a very able negotiator, but his moderating influence was lost in February, 1898, when the New York *Journal* secured and published a copy of a letter that he had written to a friend in Havana. De Lôme described McKinley as "weak and a bidder for the admiration of the crowd, besides being a would-be politician who tries to leave a door open behind himself while keeping on good terms with the jingoes of his party."

A few days later disaster struck in Havana Harbor. In late January the battleship *Maine* had come to Cuba on a courtesy call. On February 15 an explosion ripped the ship, killing some two hundred and sixty men. A naval court of inquiry reported in March that the *Maine* had been destroyed "by a submarine mine which caused the partial explosion of two or more of the forward magazines." A Spanish commission attributed the disaster to an internal explosion. Of all parties concerned, the Spanish government had the least to gain from the explosion because in the event of war Spanish defeat was almost certain. Cuban rebels, hoping for United States intervention, may have blown up the *Maine*, or it could have been an accident. In any case the American public cast aside all restraint. Trumpeted the Hearst press: "Remember the *Maine* and to hell with Spain!"

In March the President obtained from Congress a defense appropriation of fifty million dollars to use at his discretion. He told Spain that the United States wanted peace brought to Cuba immediately; implicit was a demand that the island be freed. Although Spanish leaders knew Cuba was lost, they regarded defeat in war as more honorable than surrender without a fight.

On April 9 Spain announced that the military governor of Cuba had been directed to suspend hostilities on the island. But since Spain still refused to guarantee ultimate freedom for Cuba, McKinley sent a war message to Congress. The President had no more time to negotiate; it seemed likely that Congress might declare war without waiting for him to request it. He told Congress, "The only hope of relief and repose

The Dingley Tariff of 1897 created a rigid "protection gate" for American industry, but annoyed the English. In this Judge *cartoon, President McKinley listens as John Bull threatens to "build a gate just like yours."*

from a condition which can no longer be endured is the enforced pacification of Cuba. In the name of humanity, in the name of civilization, in behalf of endangered American interests which give us the right and the duty to speak and to act, the war in Cuba must stop." McKinley deeply regretted this final step, but he believed that he had made every reasonable effort to avert war. Congress approved the declaration on April 25, 1898. The New York *Sun* proclaimed, "We are all jingoes now; and the head jingo is the Hon. William McKinley."

The United States Navy was prepared, modernization having proceeded steadily for about fifteen years. In the fall of 1897 McKinley had approved Navy Department plans to station Commodore George Dewey's Pacific fleet in Hong Kong, from where it could strike at the Spanish-held Philippine Islands. With the declaration of war, Dewey's chance came, and on May 1 he sent most of the Spanish fleet to the bottom of Manila Bay. Before the battle, few Americans knew anything about the Philippines; indeed, McKinley himself had to hunt for them on the White House globe. But the nation went wild at the news of victory.

The American assault on Cuba was carried out jointly by the Army and Navy, which was unfortunate in view of the Army's traditional state of unreadiness. Wheezing, potbellied senior officers faltered in the tropical heat. Ill-trained volunteers were rushed into action because the standing army was too small. Troops massing at Tampa, Florida, suffered from shortages of food, water, and medicine while sweltering in winter uniforms. The Army finally landed east of Santiago de Cuba in late June, and after a series of generally uninspired battles (reports to the contrary notwithstanding), pushed the Spanish back toward the city. Meanwhile, Rear Admiral William T. Sampson trapped a Spanish fleet in Santiago Bay. When the fleet attempted to escape on July 3, it was destroyed by American ships. Two weeks later the city surrendered.

On July 25 an American force landed on Puerto Rico. Late that month Spain conceded the futility of continuing the struggle. McKinley stated his terms: independence for Cuba and transfer of Puerto Rico to the United States as a war indemnity; the fate of the Philippines would be decided at a peace conference. Spain accepted these terms on August 12.

Meanwhile, events of lasting importance occurred in the Pacific. In 1897 McKinley had failed to win approval by two-thirds of the Senate of a treaty annexing the Hawaiian Islands. A year later he accomplished the same end by a joint resolution of Congress, which required only a simple majority; Hawaii was formally annexed on August 12. That same summer American forces bound for the Philippines occupied Wake Island and the Spanish island of Guam, which was later ceded to the United States.

The future of the Philippines was clearly the foremost problem at the peace conference. Judge William R. Day, who had served briefly as Secretary of State, headed the United States delegation. He favored annexing one of the islands, which would be used as a naval base. But the decision was up to McKinley, who later said, "I walked the floor of the White House night after night until midnight, and I am not ashamed to tell you . . . that I went down on my knees and prayed Almighty God for light and guidance more than one night. And one night late it came to me . . . that there was nothing left for us to do but to take them all, and to educate the Filipinos, and uplift them and civilize and Christianize them. . . ."

Spain yielded the islands after the United States agreed to a payment of twenty million dollars, but approval of the treaty by the United States Senate was not so easy. Some senators doubted that the United States had the legal right to annex the islands, and intellectuals, businessmen, and labor leaders fought the treaty. McKinley was denounced as both a tyrant and a weakling by the antiexpansionists, who were horrified that the United States, founded on the principle of democracy, would choose to govern a people without their consent. On the other hand, Indiana Senator Albert J.

Beveridge proclaimed that God "has made us the master organizers of the world to establish system where chaos reigns," and many senators sincerely felt it was time for the United States to assume international responsibilities.

Then, on February 5, the Filipinos rebelled against their American "liberators." Their action probably changed the votes of some previously antitreaty senators who were outraged by the insurrection. The treaty was ratified on February 6 by only one vote more than the two-thirds required.

The rebellion lasted three years. The United States committed 120,000 men, 1,000 of whom were killed. The insurgents, losing battle after battle, reverted to guerrilla warfare in 1900. Not until 1902 was the last rebel leader captured.

Stability and progress eventually replaced chaos in the Philippines, Puerto Rico, and Cuba. McKinley named William Howard Taft to head a commission to establish civil government in the Philippines; Taft's service was a credit to colonial government. Under the Foraker Act the United States instituted civil government in Puerto Rico. The able Major General Leonard Wood was appointed military governor of Cuba and guided the island toward self-government.

The inevitable postwar investigation of the War Department did nothing to enhance the reputation of the waspish, ineffective Secretary of War, Russell A. Alger, and McKinley eventually replaced him with Elihu Root. John Hay, an experienced, international-minded statesman, had become Secretary of State in September, 1898. A potentially dangerous scramble among several major powers for markets in China prompted Hay to win their acceptance of an Open Door policy, guaranteeing equality of commercial opportunity. A group of chauvinistic Chinese, called Boxers, bitterly resented the influence of Western culture in China. When they killed several hundred foreigners and attacked others who had sought refuge in the British legation in Peking, President McKinley attached five thousand United States soldiers to an international expeditionary force, which raised the Boxer siege.

The monetary debate was revived in 1900 with the adoption of the Gold Standard Act, supported by McKinley. This act declared the gold dollar the sole standard of currency. The gold reserve limit was raised to one hundred and fifty million dollars, and safeguards were provided to prevent the gold supply from dropping too low.

McKinley stood for re-election in 1900, though he professed that he had "had enough" of the job. Theodore Roosevelt was picked by party leaders for the Vice Presidency. Bryan, once again the Democratic nominee, spoke out for free silver and against expansionism, but McKinley had the only issue that counted—prosperity.

Prosperity continued into his second term, and social and economic problems were hidden by the glossy façade of wealth. A popular President at election time, McKinley's popularity grew even greater. He continued to study public opinion, to guide it when he could, and to appear to lead it when it formed on its own. (Representative Joseph Cannon once remarked that McKinley's ear was so close to the ground that it was full of grasshoppers.)

His wife's health remained his gravest personal problem. Although she was having fewer and fewer "good days," Ida McKinley would not be shunted aside as White House hostess. Her frequent seizures startled guests at receptions and state dinners. Her stubborn "courage" added immeasurably to her husband's burdens.

On September 5, 1901, McKinley spoke at the Pan-American Exposition. The following day he held a public reception in the Temple of Music on the exhibition grounds. Among those who attended was an anarchist, Leon Czolgosz, who carried a gun in a bandaged hand. He stepped in front of McKinley and shot him twice. His victim suffered terribly, rallied briefly, and finally succumbed to gangrene on September 14. McKinley adhered to his faith until the end. His last words to Ida were those of a favorite hymn, "Nearer, my God to Thee, Nearer to Thee."

—DONALD YOUNG

William McKinley

A PICTURE PORTFOLIO

The question posed by this political button of 1900 did not refer to tobacco but to the smokestacks of industry; McKinley promised another four years of prosperity.

FROM THE
FRONT PORCH

Advocates of McKinley's gold-standard platform of 1896 often sported handsome goldbug pins like the one above.

"The Republican Two Step and March," on the song sheet below, was one of several 1896 Republican compositions. Others included "The Honest Little Dollar's Come to Stay" and the prosaic "We Want Yer, McKinley, Yes, We Do."

While the Democratic candidate stumped the country taking his message to the multitudes, William McKinley stayed at home in Canton, Ohio, and let the multitudes come to him. From June to November of 1896 trainloads of delegations, financed by Mark Hanna's abundant campaign coffers, arrived in steady succession. Visitors were met by the Canton Home Guards, a picturesque mounted brigade, and escorted to the McKinley residence to hear the Republican candidate's views. There were two distinct advantages of such a campaign. First, it allowed the major, a Civil War veteran and two-term governor of Ohio, to maintain the proper decorum and dignity from his own front porch. As the president of a New England women's club remarked approvingly, "He does not talk wildly, and his appearance is that of a President." A second and more important advantage of the McKinley campaign was the control it gave the candidate over his audience. To avoid the embarrassment of being caught off guard, each delegation was canvassed well in advance. McKinley would request a copy of the group leader's remarks, return his carefully edited version, and prepare his response accordingly. When the delegation arrived, a member of the Home Guards would gallop ahead to alert the candidate. The ensuing confrontation held no surprises and McKinley made no slips. Yet, facing his audience "like a child looking at Santa Claus," he managed to give the whole charade a look of candid spontaneity.

Defeating William Jennings Bryan and his silver platform by a comfortable margin, the new President prepared to do battle for his high-tariff, sound-money program. With the passage of the Dingley Tariff in 1897, maintaining high protection for industry, and the Gold Standard Act of 1900, McKinley could boast fulfillment of his pledge: "Good work, good wages, and good money."

BE SURE TO SEE PAGE 32 FOR FULL DIRECTIONS.

Cut out close to work, leaving no white

BEND BACK AT
RIGHT ANGLE.

PATENTED JUNE 23ᴰ 1896

BEND BACK AT
RIGHT ANGLE
TO FORM STAND.

ART SUPPLEMENT, THE BOSTON SUNDAY GLOBE, AUGUST 23, 1896.

INTERCHANGEABLE
PRESIDENTIAL CANDIDATES.
The first Portrait is Mr. McKinley;
the second Portrait of Mr. Bryan pieces marked
B, the third Portrait of Mr. Hobart pieces marked
H, the fourth Portrait of Mr. Sewall pieces marked S,
are made by placing said lettered pieces over Mr.
McKinley's bust. One portrait at a time.
(The likeness of each at a little distance is perfect.)

The campaign cutouts above, printed in a supplement to the Boston Sunday Globe, represent the presidential and vice presidential candidates in the election of 1896. By switching the various toupees and torsos, one could create recognizable likenesses of any of the candidates: McKinley, Bryan, Hobart, or Sewall.

POWERS OF THE PRESS

EDWIN L. GODKIN

WILLIAM RANDOLPH HEARST

"To my generation," wrote William James of Edwin L. Godkin, "his was certainly the towering influence in all thought concerning public affairs." Godkin was only twenty-five when he came to America in 1856, but in England he had already established himself as a notable newspaper correspondent and man of letters. In 1865 he helped found the *Nation*, which under his editorship became the country's most powerful journal of opinion despite its small circulation. Dealing with subjects ranging from literature and the arts to politics, but especially with the problems of Negro rights and sound government, the journal was generally liberal in viewpoint. In 1883 Godkin became editor in chief of the New York *Evening Post*, a position he held until 1900, when he resigned because of failing health. A nominal Republican, Godkin displayed a strong independence and believed that national interests transcended those of party. He scored Johnson's Reconstruction programs and condemned the scandals of the Grant years. His commitment to civil reform led him to side with Tilden in the disputed election of 1876 and to lead the Mugwump faction eight years later. He favored Cleveland's fiscal ideas, but flayed his Venezuelan policy. Godkin was praised by educator Charles Eliot Norton as the nation's "soundest and best trained writer on social and economical questions."

William Randolph Hearst built a newspaper empire by refining the ore that others had mined. Noting the success of New York's yellow press, he bought the *Journal* in 1896 and soon was outsensationalizing Joseph Pulitzer's *World*. Born to wealth, Hearst began his career by taking over his father's unprofitable San Francisco *Examiner* in 1887; he turned it into a profit-making enterprise and then headed for New York. Competing against Pulitzer, Hearst successfully raided the *World* staff and used colored comic strips and supplements along with trumpeting headlines and bold, full-page editorials. The paper was frankly chauvinistic, and Hearst called the conflict with Spain "the *Journal*'s war." Hearst served two congressional terms as a Democrat, but his editorial politics fluctuated. He supported Woodrow Wilson, but scored America's entry into World War I and was firmly against the League of Nations. He backed Herbert Hoover in 1928, but came out for Franklin Roosevelt four years later—only to turn on F. D. R.'s New Deal programs. At its peak Hearst's empire included some twenty-five newspapers and numerous magazines and radio stations. His estimated gross worth in 1935 was more than two hundred million dollars, and he lived his last years in eccentric splendor at his extravagant castle, San Simeon, in California. He died in 1951.

ADOLPH S. OCHS

JOSEPH PULITZER

"It is the price of the paper, not its character, that will change," said Adolph S. Ochs, publisher of *The New York Times*, in 1898. Ochs had taken over the impoverished paper two years before; because of its inability to cover the war with Spain as fully as its rich competition, its popularity had not increased. So Ochs gambled. Strongly advised to the contrary and ridiculed by rival sheets, he lowered the price of the *Times* from three cents to a penny. Circulation and advertising shot up, and Ochs proved that there was a market for a "clean, dignified and trustworthy" newspaper even in the heyday of yellow journalism. *The New York Times* was not the first paper the Cincinnati-born Ochs had resuscitated. In 1878, at twenty, he had bought controlling interest in the Chattanooga *Times* for $250. He won a large readership by refusing questionable advertising and by subordinating editorial content to thorough, accurate news copy. In New York Ochs's slogan was "All the news that's fit to print." Throughout his life he maintained his standards of scrupulous, unsensational, in-depth reporting and took great pride in *The New York Times*'s status as a "newspaper of record." He favored sound money, tariff reform, and low taxes, but was not a mouthpiece for any political party or faction. Adolph Ochs was seventy-seven years old when he died in Chattanooga in 1935.

"THE ROYAL FEAST OF BELSHAZZAR BLAINE AND THE MONEY KINGS," screamed the New York *World* during the presidential campaign of 1884. It was a typical *World* headline, reflecting the political and journalistic philosophies of the paper's publisher, Joseph Pulitzer. He had bought the *World* from Jay Gould the year before, and through blaring banners, numerous features and cartoons, and heavy emphasis on crime, scandal, and catastrophe, had become, wrote one historian, "the first publisher to reach a truly massive audience." While the *World*'s news columns appealed to the common man, its editorial pages were aimed at the liberal intelligentsia. After the collapse of the Liberal Republican movement Pulitzer became a staunch Democrat, advocating civil reform and sound money. Hungarian-born, he had emigrated in 1864 and had served in the Union army. He began his newspaper career in St. Louis, where he arranged the merger that produced the successful St. Louis *Post-Dispatch*. In the 1890's the fierce rivalry between the papers run by Hearst and Pulitzer helped generate public desire for war with Spain, but the *World* eventually dropped its sensational format and became the nation's leading Democratic organ. In his will Pulitzer established a journalism school at New York's Columbia University and provided for the annual awarding of Pulitzer Prizes.

647

$50,000 REWARD.—WHO DESTROYED THE MAINE?—$50,000 REWARD.

EDITION FOR GREATER NEW YORK.

NEW YORK JOURNAL
AND ADVERTISER.

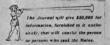

The Journal will give $50,000 for information, furnished to it exclusively, that will convict the person or persons who sank the Maine.

The Journal will give $50,000 for information, furnished to it exclusively, that will convict the person or persons who sank the Maine.

NO. 5,572. Copyright, 1898, by W. R. Hearst—NEW YORK, THURSDAY, FEBRUARY 17, 1898.—16 PAGES. PRICE ONE CENT in Greater New York | Elsewhere and Jersey City—TWO CENTS.

DESTRUCTION OF THE WAR SHIP MAINE WAS THE WORK OF AN ENEMY.

$50,000!
$50,000 REWARD!
For the Detection of the Perpetrator of the Maine Outrage!

The New York Journal hereby offers a reward of $50,000 CASH for information, FURNISHED TO IT EXCLUSIVELY, which shall lead to the detection and conviction of the person, persons or government criminally responsible for the explosion which resulted in the destruction, at Havana, of the United States war ship Maine and the loss of 258 lives of American sailors.

The $50,000 CASH offered for the above information is on deposit with Wells, Fargo & Co.

No one is barred, be he the humble fort misguided woman sking out a few miserable dollars by acting as a spy, or the attaché of a government secret service, plotting, by any devilish means, to revenge fancied insults or cripple menacing countries.

This offer has been cabled to Europe and will be made public in every capital of the Continent and in London this morning.

The Journal believes that any man who can be bought to commit murder can also be bought to betray his comrades. FOR THE PERPETRATOR OF THIS OUTRAGE HAD ACCOMPLICES.

W. R. HEARST.

Assistant Secretary Roosevelt Convinced the Explosion of the War Ship Was Not an Accident.

The Journal Offers $50,000 Reward for the Conviction of the Criminals Who Sent 258 American Sailors to Their Death. Naval Officers Unanimous That the Ship Was Destroyed on Purpose.

$50,000!
$50,000 REWARD!
For the Detection of the Perpetrator of the Maine Outrage!

The New York Journal hereby offers a reward of $50,000 CASH for information, FURNISHED TO IT EXCLUSIVELY, which shall lead to the detection and conviction of the person, persons or government criminally responsible for the explosion which resulted in the destruction, at Havana, of the United States war ship Maine and the loss of 258 lives of American sailors.

The $50,000 CASH offered for the above information is on deposit with Wells, Fargo & Co.

No one is barred, be he the humble fort misguided woman, sking out a few miserable dollars by acting as a spy, or the attaché of a government secret service, plotting, by any devilish means, to revenge fancied insults or cripple menacing countries.

This offer has been cabled to Europe and will be made public in every capital of the Continent and in London this morning.

The Journal believes that any man who can be bought to commit murder can also be bought to betray his comrades. FOR THE PERPETRATOR OF THIS OUTRAGE HAD ACCOMPLICES.

W. R. HEARST.

NAVAL OFFICERS THINK THE MAINE WAS DESTROYED BY A SPANISH MINE.

George Eugene Bryson, the Journal's special correspondent at Havana, cables that it is the secret opinion of many Spaniards in the Cuban capital that the Maine was destroyed and 258 of her men killed by means of a submarine mine, or fixed torpedo. This is the opinion of several American naval authorities. The Spaniards, it is believed, arranged to have the Maine anchored over one of the harbor mines. Wires connected the mine with a powder magazine, and it is thought the explosion was caused by sending an electric current through the wire. If this can be proven, the brutal nature of the Spaniards will be shown by the fact that they waited to spring the mine until after all the men had retired for the night. The Maltese cross in the picture shows where the mine may have been fired.

Hidden Mine or a Sunken Torpedo Believed to Have Been the Weapon Used Against the American Man-of-War---Officers and Men Tell Thrilling Stories of Being Blown Into the Air Amid a Mass of Shattered Steel and Exploding Shells---Survivors Brought to Key West Scout the Idea of Accident---Spanish Officials Protest Too Much---Our Cabinet Orders a Searching Inquiry---Journal Sends Divers to Havana to Report Upon the Condition of the Wreck.
Was the Vessel Anchored Over a Mine?

BY CAPTAIN E. L. ZALINSKI, U. S. A.

(Captain Zalinski is the inventor of the famous dynamite gun, which would be the principal factor in our coast defence in case of war.)

Assistant Secretary of the Navy Theodore Roosevelt says he is convinced that the destruction of the Maine in Havana Harbor was not an accident.

The Journal offers a reward of $50,000 for exclusive evidence that will convict the person, persons or Government criminally responsible for the destruction of the American battle ship and the death of 258 of its crew.

The suspicion that the Maine was deliberately blown up grows stronger every hour. Not a single fact to the contrary has been produced.

Captain Sigsbee, of the Maine, and Consul-General Lee both urge that public opinion be suspended until they have completed their investigation. They are taking the course of tactful men who are convinced that there has been treachery.

Washington reports very late that Captain Sigsbee had feared some such event as a hidden mine. The English cipher code was used all day yesterday b the naval officers in cabling instead of the usual American code.

The question of who sank the Maine was purely academic in the face of press sensationalism and public clamor for war with Spain. As McKinley vacillated, New York Republican Teddy Roosevelt charged that he "had no more backbone than a chocolate eclair." Public sentiment prevailed and the President declared war.

WAR WITH SPAIN

Thirteen months after McKinley's inauguration, America was at war with Spain. Indignation—fanned by immoderate newspapers—over Spanish oppression in Cuba had long been simmering, but the sinking of the U.S.S. *Maine* in Havana Harbor was the event that prompted the declaration of war in April, 1898. That May, Commodore Dewey eliminated Spanish power in the Philippines, and in June a joint Army-Navy expedition set out to liberate Cuba. While Admiral William T. Sampson held the Spanish fleet in Santiago Bay, General William R. Shafter's land force pushed in to take the port through a series of battles in the surrounding heights. On July 1, some 7,000 United States troops defeated an enemy force of about 600 at the village of El Caney, losing 441 men as against 235 Spanish casualties. One lieutenant described the confusion in American lines: "The bullets . . . are raining into our very faces. A soldier comes running up, and cries out, 'Lieutenant, we're shooting into our own men!'" Meanwhile other American troops—including Teddy Roosevelt's Rough Riders—were charging up San Juan Hill in an assault that increased American casualties to almost 1,600. From their newly won vantage point Shafter's men trained their guns on Santiago Bay. On July 3 the Spanish fleet tried to escape, but was pursued and destroyed by Admiral Sampson's superior naval force. The "war of liberation" was over.

CHICAGO HISTORICAL SOCIETY

The Kurz & Allison lithograph above depicts in vivid detail the American siege of El Caney and the Spanish fortifications in the heights above Santiago. In the distance lies the Spanish fleet, bottled up in the bay by an American naval blockade. The destruction of the fleet brought the Spanish-American War to a quick end.

AN AMERICAN EMPIRE

The taste of Empire is in the mouth of the people even as the taste of blood in the jungle," proclaimed the Washington *Post* before the outbreak of the Spanish-American War. Whetting the public appetite, President McKinley announced that "when the war is over, we must keep what we want." In the peace that followed, Cuba was granted independence and the United States took over Guam, Puerto Rico, and the Philippines. Expansion was not confined to the spoils of war. Hawaii was annexed in 1898, and Wake Island was also formally occupied. When the islands of Samoa were divided between the United States and Germany in 1899, the press announced proudly, "We have emerged in undisputed possession of the best of that group of islands." American influence in China was reflected in the Open Door trade policy and its unfortunate aftermath, the Boxer Rebellion of 1900, during which American troops joined an expedition sent to rescue besieged foreigners in Peking. In the presidential election of that year the issue of imperialism dominated the Republican platform. McKinley—and imperialism—won the nation's mandate. But as his friend Charles Dawes noted, "The President seems more impressed with his responsibilities than his triumph."

The Battle of Manila Bay in 1898 inspired the handsome Japanese print above. On May 1, Commodore George Dewey entered the bay, delivered a scathing broadside, and destroyed the Spanish squadron. With the fall of Manila in August, the United States proclaimed military occupation of the Philippines.

Filipino insurrectionist Emilio Aguinaldo was against trading Spanish domination for American control. When the United States failed to grant independence, he led the islanders in armed revolt. In the photograph at left, American soldiers dig in for a bloody three-year guerrilla war against the elusive natives.

651

MEN AROUND McKINLEY

THE PHILLIPS GALLERY

ELIHU ROOT

"Thank the President for me," replied Elihu Root when offered the position of Secretary of War, "but say that it is quite absurd. I know nothing about war. . . ." Informed, however, that McKinley was looking for "a lawyer to direct the government of these Spanish islands," Root, a New York corporation lawyer, agreed to accept the Cabinet post. Taking office in 1899, he formulated policies for the administration of Cuba, the Philippines, and other new colonial possessions. Stressing rehabilitation, the guarantee of individual liberties, development of local institutions, and protection of United States interests, he laid the foundations of American imperialism. Before he resigned in 1904 he reorganized the Army and created the Army War College. As Secretary of State under Roosevelt from 1905 to 1909, Root worked to develop friendly relations with Latin America and Japan; his efforts won him the Nobel Peace Prize in 1912. From 1909 to 1915 he served in the United States Senate. Critical of American neutrality at the beginning of World War I, he favored—with reservations—United States membership in the League of Nations. He also advocated membership in the Permanent Court of International Peace. President of the Carnegie Endowment for International Peace, Root was a respected elder statesman until his death at ninety-one in 1937.

BROWN BROTHERS

MARCUS A. HANNA

"I love McKinley!" declared Republican party leader Marcus A. Hanna. "He is the best man I ever knew." A hardheaded realist with few political scruples, Hanna was attracted by McKinley's idealism. An Ohio capitalist whose interests included the Cleveland *Herald*, the Cleveland Opera House, and control of Cleveland's street railway system, Hanna saw political power chiefly as a means to promote big business. McKinley, he felt, lent the proper touch of ideology to his cause. In 1891 he supported McKinley for governor, worked for his re-election in 1893, and began grooming him for the Presidency in 1896. Advertising him as the "advance agent of prosperity," Hanna secured the nomination for his candidate on the first ballot. Hanna became chairman of the Republican National Committee and raised several million dollars to assure McKinley's election. Appointed to the Senate in 1896, Hanna served as the President's most intimate adviser. Although still a champion of large corporate enterprise, he also defended labor's right to organize. Upon Theodore Roosevelt's succession to the Presidency in 1901, Hanna continued in the role of adviser and helped to settle labor disputes in the anthracite coal industry. Hanna might have become a presidential candidate himself had not his death in 1904 terminated a growing Mark Hanna-for-President movement.

GEORGE DEWEY

When Admiral George Dewey returned from the Spanish-American War in 1899, he was welcomed as a national hero. An Annapolis graduate who had served under David Farragut in the Civil War, Dewey became chief of the Navy Department's Bureau of Equipment in 1889 and president of the Board of Inspection six years later. Promoted to commodore, he assumed command of the Asiatic squadron in 1897. His cool heroics during the ensuing conflict with Spain are legendary. Approaching the enemy guns in Manila Bay, the commander gave the laconic order, "You may fire when ready, Gridley." Dewey went on to victory, annihilating the Spanish squadron, taking the Philippines, and eliminating Spanish naval power in the Far East. A grateful Congress created the rank of admiral of the Navy for him. Returning home a year after his spectacular victory, he was greeted hysterically by the nation. There were Dewey songs, Dewey banners, Dewey neckties, Dewey hatpins, Dewey rattles, and a gum called Dewey chewies. The American public launched a brief Dewey-for-President boom that failed to mature sufficiently, however, to bring him a nomination. In 1900 Admiral Dewey was appointed president of the General Board of the Navy Department and served in that position until his death at the age of seventy-nine on January 16, 1917.

JOHN M. HAY

John M. Hay's record as a statesman was, President McKinley said, "one of the most important and interesting pages of our diplomatic history." Trained as a lawyer, Hay left Springfield, Illinois, in his early twenties to act as assistant private secretary to President-elect Abraham Lincoln, whom he served until 1865. After traveling abroad as a diplomat, he returned to the United States in 1870 and became a writer on the New York *Tribune*. Hay served as assistant secretary of state from 1879 to 1881, and in 1897 he was appointed ambassador to Great Britain by McKinley. Named Secretary of State after the outbreak of the Spanish-American War in 1898, he supported President McKinley's policy of American rule in the Philippines. In 1899 he backed the Open Door policy in China and was largely responsible for the preservation of China's territorial integrity during the Boxer Rebellion of 1900. Retaining his post under Theodore Roosevelt, Hay settled the Alaskan boundary dispute in 1903 and concluded the important Hay-Pauncefote Treaty with Britain, which cleared the way for construction of the Panama Canal. Hay was a poet, novelist, and historian as well as a diplomat. Among his published works are *Pike County Ballads*, *Castilian Days*, *The Bread-Winners*, and the ten-volume *Abraham Lincoln: A History*, which he wrote with John Nicolay in 1890.

The Issue — 1900
·LIBERTY·
·JUSTICE·
·HUMANITY·

1776 LIBERTY

1900 NO IMPERIALISM.

W.J.BRYAN

NO CROWN OF THORNS

NO CROSS OF GOLD

DECLARATION OF INDEPENDENCE

DOLLAR OF THE DADDIES

16 TO 1

TRUSTS

"GIVE US LIBERTY OR GIVE US DEATH"

EQUAL RIGHTS TO ALL   SPECIAL PRIVILEGES TO NONE.

COPYRIGHT 1900
BY
NEVILLE WILLIAMS

TRUTH AND
ELOQUENCE

In 1900 William Jennings Bryan campaigned against McKinley for a second time. Four years had not changed the silver Democrat's views. Except for the new issue of expansion, Bryan might have used his campaign notes from 1896. To the gold-standard adherents in that year he had hurled his famous protest: "You shall not crucify mankind upon a cross of gold." Despite evidence that the gold standard had bolstered the American economy, he continued to call for free coinage of silver as a panacea for the ills of the masses. Bryan saw the campaign as more than a contest of politics and economics. "Every political . . . [and] economic question," he asserted, "is in reality a great moral question." To Bryan it was a contest between good and evil; a class struggle between the "toiling masses" and the big money interests supported by President McKinley.

Bryan's political convictions were rooted in the heritage of his native Middle West. Born in Salem, Illinois, in 1860, he was reared in an agrarian society that stressed Protestant morality, the dignity of the laborer, and government by majority rule. With these ideals the young lawyer moved to Nebraska, where he slipped easily and naturally into local politics, soon establishing a reputation as "the silver-tongued orator from Nebraska." Elected to Congress in 1890, he spoke against the protective tariff and repeal of the silver-purchase law. The Democratic candidate in 1896 and 1900, he campaigned against McKinley as the representative of the common man. One admirer commented that Bryan spoke with an "entire lack of artfulness [that] makes him invincible." But he was not invincible; he lost the first election on the silver issue and the second on the question of expansion. However admirable his anti-imperialist convic-

tions may have been, they were out of harmony with a nation eager to claim the spoils of the Spanish-American War. In 1908 Bryan ran against William Howard Taft—his third and last try for the Presidency. Continuing as a leader of the Democratic party, he kept his ideas before the people through lecture tours and editorials in the *Commoner*, a weekly newspaper that he published from 1901 to 1913. In 1912 he supported Woodrow Wilson, who appointed him Secretary of State. Unable to reconcile his pacifist convictions with United States involvement in World War I, Bryan resigned in 1915.

A pathetic incident marked the end of his career. Shortly before his death in 1925 he became involved in the prosecution of John T. Scopes, indicted for teaching the theory of evolution, which was banned by law from the Tennessee public schools. Bryan, a fundamentalist who had helped to draft such legislation, was subjected to a withering cross-examination by Clarence Darrow that revealed the narrowness of his religious dogma and the limitations of his scientific thought. But Bryan was then a man of sixty-five. At the height of his powers he had expressed unbounded faith in the progress of mankind. "He believes the world is getting better all the time," observed the editor of a Western daily, "and it is impossible to be around him a great deal without sharing his hopeful view of things." To some, William Jennings Bryan appeared to be the "incarnation of demagogy, the apotheosis of riot [and] destruction," and his editorials in the *Commoner* were denounced as an attempt to create dissension between the poor and the rich. But to thousands of others he represented the twin virtues "Truth" and "Eloquence"; to the "plain people" of America he was, as one Nebraskan put it, "the brightest and purest advocate of our cause. . . ."

William Jennings Bryan (left), on a 1900 campaign poster

The 1900 campaign button above shows McKinley and his new running mate, Teddy Roosevelt, who soon succeeded him.

The President delivered his last speech (right) the day before his assassination.

A group of silent mourners thronged the streets of McKinley's home town, Canton, Ohio, as the President's

ASSASSINATION

On September 6, 1901, during a public reception at the Pan-American Exposition in Buffalo, New York, President William McKinley was shot by a vacant-eyed, twenty-eight-year-old anarchist named Leon Czolgosz. Three years earlier, the assassin had suffered a breakdown, left his factory job in Cleveland, and retired to the bleak Ohio farm on which his family lived. Restless and despondent, he moved to Buffalo in the summer of 1901. Hearing of the President's visit, he bought a revolver, walked into the reception, and fired two shots into McKinley's chest and stomach. A nondescript, antisocial outcast, Czolgosz was the complete opposite of the public idol who had stood but a few feet in front of him, unaware of his existence. "I didn't believe one man should have so much service," the assassin said later, "and another man should have none." The President was rushed to an emergency hospital on the exposition grounds, but the second bullet, which had ripped the stomach walls, was never located by the doctors. The lighting in the operating room was inadequate, and the wound was sewn up, without proper drainage, with the aid of the setting sun and a reflecting mirror. McKinley rallied briefly, and on September 7 a medical bulletin assured the worried public that "no serious symptoms have developed." Within a few days, however, a gangrenous infection set in. On the evening of September 14, the physician attending William McKinley announced the tragic news to the nation: "The President is dead."

remains were removed from the church. It was the end of a tragic procession that had begun in Buffalo.

FACTS IN SUMMARY: WILLIAM McKINLEY

CHRONOLOGY

UNITED STATES		McKINLEY
	1843	Born January 29
Texas annexed	1845	
Mexican War begins	1846	
Taylor elected President		
Fillmore becomes President	1850	
Compromise of 1850		
Pierce elected President	1852	
Kansas-Nebraska Act	1854	
Buchanan inaugurated as President	1857	
Dred Scott decision		
Lincoln elected President	1860	Enters Allegheny College
South Carolina secedes		
Fort Sumter fired upon	1861	Enlists in Army
Battle of Antietam	1862	Fights at Antietam
		Promoted to first lieutenant
Emancipation Proclamation	1863	
Battle of Gettysburg		
Lee surrenders at Appomattox	1865	Promoted to brevet major
Lincoln assassinated		
	1866	Enters Albany Law School
	1867	Graduates from law school
		Moves to Canton, Ohio
Fourteenth Amendment ratified	1868	Elected president of Canton Y.M.C.A.
	1869	Elected county prosecuting attorney
	1871	Marries Ida Saxton
	1876	Elected to U.S. House of Representatives
Hayes elected President	1877	
	1878	Votes for Bland-Allison bill
Garfield elected President	1880	Re-elected to Congress
		Made temporary chairman of Ohio Republican convention
Cleveland elected President	1884	Made permanent chairman of Ohio convention
Hatch Act	1887	
Benjamin Harrison elected President	1888	
	1889	Becomes chairman of House Ways and Means Committee
Sherman Antitrust Act	1890	Sponsors McKinley tariff bill
	1891	Elected governor of Ohio
	1893	Re-elected governor
	1896	Elected President

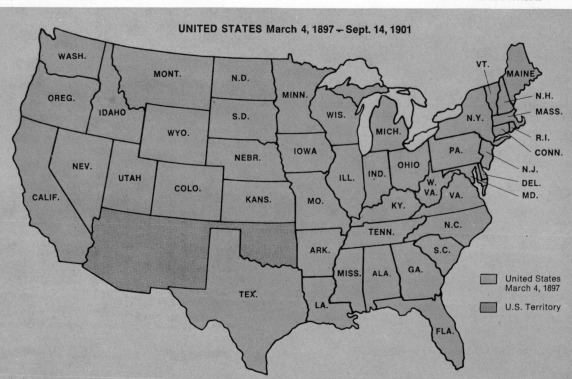

UNITED STATES March 4, 1897 – Sept. 14, 1901

- United States March 4, 1897
- U.S. Territory

Dingley Tariff	1897	
Sinking of the *Maine*	1898	*Declares war with Spain*
Spanish-American War		*Demands cession of*
Annexation of Hawaii		*Philippines*
Treaty of Paris		
Open Door policy	1899	
First Hague Conference		
Partition of Samoa		
Currency Act	1900	*Re-elected President*
Boxer Rebellion		
	1901	*Appoints Taft civil governor of Philippines*
		Shot September 6
		Dies September 14

BIOGRAPHICAL FACTS

BIRTH: Niles, Ohio, Jan. 29, 1843

ANCESTRY: Scotch-Irish and English

FATHER: William McKinley; b. Pine Township, Pa., Nov. 15, 1807; d. Canton, Ohio, Nov. 24, 1892

FATHER'S OCCUPATION: Iron-founder

MOTHER: Nancy Allison McKinley; b. New Lisbon, Ohio, April 22, 1809; d. Canton, Ohio, Dec. 12, 1897

BROTHERS: David Allison (1829–1892); James (?–1889); Abner (1849–1904)

SISTERS: Anna (1832–1890); Mary; Helen; Sarah Elizabeth

WIFE: Ida Saxton; b. Canton, Ohio, June 8, 1847; d. Canton, Ohio, May 26, 1907

MARRIAGE: Canton, Ohio, Jan. 25, 1871

CHILDREN: Katherine (1871–1875); Ida (1873–1873)

EDUCATION: Attended Poland Academy, Ohio, and Allegheny College

RELIGIOUS AFFILIATION: Methodist

OCCUPATIONS BEFORE PRESIDENCY: Teacher; soldier; lawyer

MILITARY SERVICE: Joined Ohio 23rd Volunteers in 1861; rose to rank of major before leaving Army in 1865

PRE-PRESIDENTIAL OFFICES: Member of U.S. House of Representatives; Governor of Ohio

AGE AT INAUGURATION: 54

DEATH: Buffalo, N.Y., Sept. 14, 1901

PLACE OF BURIAL: Canton, Ohio

ELECTION OF 1896

CANDIDATES	ELECTORAL VOTE	POPULAR VOTE
William McKinley Republican	271	7,102,246
William J. Bryan Democratic	176	6,492,559
John M. Palmer National Democratic	—	133,148
Joshua Levering Prohibition	—	132,007

FIRST ADMINISTRATION

INAUGURATION: March 4, 1897; the Capitol, Washington, D.C.

VICE PRESIDENT: Garret A. Hobart

SECRETARY OF STATE: John Sherman; William R. Day (from April 28, 1898); John Hay (from Sept. 30, 1898)

SECRETARY OF THE TREASURY: Lyman J. Gage

SECRETARY OF WAR: Russell A. Alger; Elihu Root (from Aug. 1, 1899)

ATTORNEY GENERAL: Joseph McKenna; John W. Griggs (from Feb. 1, 1898)

POSTMASTER GENERAL: James A. Gary; Charles Emory Smith (from April 21, 1898)

SECRETARY OF THE NAVY: John D. Long

SECRETARY OF THE INTERIOR: Cornelius N. Bliss; Ethan A. Hitchcock (from Feb. 20, 1899)

SECRETARY OF AGRICULTURE: James Wilson

SUPREME COURT APPOINTMENT: Joseph McKenna (1898)

55th CONGRESS (March 4, 1897–March 4, 1899):
Senate: 47 Republicans; 34 Democrats; 7 Others
House: 204 Republicans; 113 Democrats; 40 Others

56th CONGRESS (March 4, 1899–March 4, 1901):
Senate: 53 Republicans; 26 Democrats; 8 Others
House: 185 Republicans; 163 Democrats; 9 Others

ELECTION OF 1900

CANDIDATES	ELECTORAL VOTE	POPULAR VOTE
William McKinley Republican	292	7,218,491
William J. Bryan Democratic	155	6,356,734
John C. Wooley Prohibition	—	208,914
Eugene V. Debs Socialist	—	87,814

SECOND ADMINISTRATION

INAUGURATION: March 4, 1901; the Capitol, Washington, D.C.

VICE PRESIDENT: Theodore Roosevelt

SECRETARY OF STATE: John Hay

SECRETARY OF THE TREASURY: Lyman J. Gage

SECRETARY OF WAR: Elihu Root

ATTORNEY GENERAL: John W. Griggs; Philander C. Knox (from April 10, 1901)

POSTMASTER GENERAL: Charles Emory Smith

SECRETARY OF THE NAVY: John D. Long

SECRETARY OF THE INTERIOR: Ethan A. Hitchcock

SECRETARY OF AGRICULTURE: James Wilson

57th CONGRESS (March 4, 1901–March 4, 1903):
Senate: 55 Republicans; 31 Democrats; 4 Others
House: 197 Republicans; 151 Democrats; 9 Others

THEODORE ROOSEVELT

Theodore Roosevelt of New York could not have been less like his predecessor in the White House. If McKinley had been the archetype of standpat conservatism, Teddy Roosevelt epitomized a brash new breed of political activists. Never sit still, Roosevelt declared. "Get action, do things . . . take a place wherever you are and be somebody. . . ." Hunter and scholar, rancher and soldier, black-tie patrician and reformer, he was a man of volcanic energy. Heedless of precedent, responsive to the new needs and conflicts of a nation expanding industrially and asserting its rank in the world, he was a prime mover in shaping the Presidency as we know it today: a mediating, countervailing force in American affairs; the embodiment of national unity above section, interest, and class; the ultimate custodian of the general good.

"Teedie" Roosevelt was born on October 27, 1858, at 28 East 20th Street in New York City. His grandfather, Cornelius Van Schaack Roosevelt, was an entrepreneur and investor who ranked with Cornelius Vanderbilt and William B. Astor among New York tycoons. Teedie's father, Theodore, Sr.—whom his son considered "the best man I ever knew"—was a prospering glass importer who had substantial banking interests; he was an active Lincoln Republican and a philanthropic Presbyterian. "Take care of your morals first, your health next," he advised Teedie, "and finally your studies." Teedie's mother was Martha Bulloch, an aristocratic Georgian who, despite her husband's friendship with Lincoln, remained loyal to the South during the Civil War. It was a lively family, including three children besides Theodore.

"Nothing in this world is worth having or worth doing," an older T. R. declared, "unless it means effort, pain, difficulty. . . ." Roosevelt's childhood, despite the comforts of wealth and status, gave the future President great

Theodore Roosevelt, painted in 1903 by John Singer Sargent

661

Roosevelt's birthplace in New York, shown as it was during his youth, is now a museum open to the public.

pain indeed. Frail, nearsighted, wracked by asthma, the boy was confined to a life of private tutors and close supervision. He could remember his father "carrying me in my distress, in my battles for breath, up and down a room all night. . . . I could breathe, I could sleep, when he had me in his arms." Teedie turned inward, read widely and voraciously, and cultivated an abiding interest in natural science, turning his bedroom into a museum of insects and stuffed birds.

En route to Maine's Moosehead Lake after an asthma attack at the age of thirteen, T. R. was taunted by two bullies for his city manners. The bespectacled lad flew into a rage and, fists flying, went at his tormentors—to no avail. Humiliated, Roosevelt vowed to build his strength. In a home gymnasium he took to bar bell and punching bag, building up his muscles. "There were all kinds of things of which I was afraid at first," he later confessed, ". . . but by acting as if I was not afraid I gradually ceased to be afraid." It was a triumph of will over trauma, confirming in Roosevelt a chip-on-the-shoulder truculence that would both ennoble and beset him throughout life. "Don't hit at all if it is honorably possible to avoid hitting," he would say, "but *never* hit soft."

Preparation for college required intense study after Roosevelt's spotty succession of tutors. But at eighteen he was ready for Harvard, where, he said loftily, his aim was to become a naturalist like Audubon. In Cambridge he lamented that few of his classmates had come there "with the idea of getting an education." Roosevelt himself was a serious scholar, graduating twenty-first in a class of 177. In his senior year he began work on his book *The Naval War of 1812*, a study he preferred to more classical disciplines. But his interest in naval history and natural science did not preclude other activities. He boxed—and boxed hard—in the college gym. Sideburned and dressed to the nines, he hobnobbed with Boston's Brahmins, from whose ranks he picked a bride, Alice Hathaway Lee. Married in 1880, the year of T. R.'s graduation, they moved in with the elder Theodore, who would soon leave his son an inheritance of two hundred thousand dollars.

At Columbia Law School T. R. discovered a distaste for the law. But he remained in school, seeking diversion by joining the National Guard, riding horseback through

Central Park, attending all the big parties, and, while on vacation, scaling the Matterhorn. Itching for action in 1881, he joined New York City's Twenty-first District Republican Club, an organization staffed by ward heelers. Assured by his friends that politics was a muddying business run by society's lowest elements, T. R. replied: "If this were so, it merely meant that the people I knew did not belong to the governing class . . . and that I intended to be one of the governing class."

Thus turning his back on his peers, Roosevelt, at twenty-three, entered the lists of state politics and won the Twenty-first District's seat in the New York assembly. He already looked as he is now remembered: thick-necked and clamp-jawed; with large teeth and piercing blue eyes framed by pince-nez; agile, wiry, and nervous. Roosevelt's boyish, high-pitched voice was promptly heard in the chambers of Albany as the fledgling solon arose to accuse financier Jay Gould of attempting to corrupt a New York State supreme court judge. Urging that the judge be impeached, T. R. thundered his classic charge that Gould was "part of that most dangerous of all dangerous classes, the wealthy criminal class." They were bitter words for the Albany old guard to swallow, and Teddy was contemptuously christened a Harvard "goo-goo," or one committed to good government.

T. R.'s reform record in Albany, however, was equivocal. It is true that after inspecting the sweatshops of New York's cigar industry he voted to abolish them and that he voted to limit the factory workday of women and children. But it is also true that he refused to support prison reform and opposed attempts to tighten enforcement of New York's eight-hour law and to limit to twelve hours the workday of street railway drivers.

Tragedy hit the Roosevelt family in February, 1884, when T. R.'s mother died of typhoid fever and his young wife died of Bright's disease two days after giving birth to a child. Inconsolable, Roosevelt left his infant daughter, Alice, and headed west to the wild Dakota Territory, seeking a con-

quest of sorrow through "the strenuous life . . . of labor and strife." In the Badlands, branding steers and breaking stampedes at the Elkhorn Ranch, in which he had invested in 1883, T. R. gained strength and confidence. There is no doubt that he won the respect of his ranch hands, despite their initial derision of him as a "four-eyed tenderfoot." Although given to patrician commands, such as "Hasten forward quickly," he could ride herd with the best of them.

Returning to the East, T. R. placed third in an 1886 bid for the New York mayoralty. His disappointment was assuaged in December by his marriage to Edith Kermit Carow, who was to bear him five children.

Political service to Benjamin Harrison won Roosevelt a seat on the United States Civil Service Commission in 1889—a post of scant intrinsic consequence through which T. R., nevertheless, gained national attention. While commissioner, T. R. said with one eye on the press, he would uphold the merit system and "let the chips fall where they will." He spotted blackmail in the New York Custom House and fought campaign assessments of federal workers. Reappointed by Democrat Grover Cleveland, he removed thousands of federal jobs from political patronage before his retirement in 1895.

Appointed New York City police commissioner by reform Mayor William L. Strong that same year, T. R. again courted headlines. Fighting both Democrats and Republicans, he established a merit system of police appointment and promotion. He helped condemn tenements, fought graft, supported social work, and pounded the precincts until dawn to keep police on their toes. But his handling of strikes did not endear him to the oppressed: "The mob takes its own chance," he declared. "Order will be kept at whatever cost."

A reluctant President McKinley yielded to pressure and appointed Roosevelt assistant secretary of the Navy in 1897. Under permissive Secretary John Long, Roosevelt again seized every chance to thrust himself forward. An overt imperialist and a disciple of Alfred Thayer Mahan's theory of naval supremacy as a key to power, he favored the direct annexation of Hawaii as a foil to Japanese expansion and hailed territorial conquest as a hallmark of racial superiority over the "weak and craven." He thought a direct assault upon Spanish-held Cuba would be "a bully war."

On February 25, 1898, during Secretary Long's absence of a day, T. R. boldly cabled Admiral Dewey in the Pacific, ordering the fleet to Hong Kong. "In the event of declaration of war [against] Spain," he ordered, "your duty will be to see that the Spanish squadron does not leave the Asiatic coast, and then offensive operations in Philippine Islands." T. R.'s act, however insubordinate, helped assure American victory in Manila Bay.

Angered by the sinking of the *Maine*, Roosevelt resigned on May 6, 1898, to do battle on the field. With his friend Leonard Wood he rounded up an improbable band of sportsmen, Texas Rangers, and other cronies and whipped them into shape as the First U.S. Volunteer Cavalry Regiment, the renowned "Rough Riders." How much they contributed to the American expeditionary effort in Cuba remains open to question, but there is no doubt of T. R.'s personal courage in leading his men in the teeth of Spanish fire. He emerged from the war a hero.

Roosevelt's great political potential was quickly exploited by New York's Republican bosses, who badly needed a winning candidate for governor. Senator Thomas Platt, high priest of the party and staunch friend of big business, did not like Roosevelt, branding him an "altruist," using the word, said T. R., "as a term of reproach, as if it was Communistic. . . ." Adroit at political arithmetic, however, and persuaded that T. R. could be controlled, Platt permitted Roosevelt's nomination for governor. In a strenuous whistle-stop tour of the state, a Rough Rider escort noisily at his elbow, Roosevelt won the governorship for the G.O.P. by a shaky margin of 18,000 votes. He was now "Teddy" to the public—a name he disliked—and one of the most talked-about politicians in the United States.

Taking office in January, 1899, Governor Roosevelt quickly put Platt in his place. While avoiding an open break, he told Platt that he was the boss, that he would make his own appointments and pursue his own policies of reform. Opposed not only by big-business Republicans but by those he dismissed as "conservative Democrats of the Wall Street type," T. R. appealed directly to the people. Scarcely a radical, he derided reformers "who bathed every day, and didn't steal, but whose only good point was 'respectability'. . . ." His motto was a West African hunting proverb: "Speak softly and carry a big stick; you will go far."

T. R.'s voice, however, could be heard all over Albany. Infuriating Platt, Roosevelt tightened laws regulating sweatshops, pushed for closer supervision of utilities and insurance companies, forced reform in the handling of food and drugs, and sponsored regulations of the workday for women and children. And when labor riots threatened the public safety at the Croton dam, he ordered the state militia to stand by.

T. R.'s greatest victory as governor came with the legislature's passage of a state tax on corporation franchises. The conversion of New York streetcars from horsepower to electricity had afforded venal businessmen and politicians a field day for what Roosevelt condemned as "down-right bribery." Franchises were awarded on the basis of favoritism and kickbacks. But Governor Roosevelt insisted, as "a matter of plain decency and honesty," that corporation franchises be taxed. Platt was furious, and a dutiful legislature dallied, refusing even to introduce, let alone vote on, T. R.'s franchise bill. Only when the governor threatened to march to the assembly and read the bill out himself did the lawmakers, conscious of the public storm Roosevelt had kicked up, put the bill through.

T. R.'s Albany victory won national attention. But if the people hailed a dramatic new advocate in Theodore Roosevelt, Platt and his coadjutors in the G.O.P. most surely did not. "I want to get rid of the bastard," Platt thundered. "I don't want him raising

This cartoon of 1900 shows the regional maidens enticing Roosevelt into vice presidential waters.

hell in my state any longer." So the bosses schemed, torn between a desire to get T. R. out of their hair and a wish to exploit his vote-getting vigor. Their solution: bury the troublemaker in the Vice Presidency.

President McKinley was cool to the idea of Roosevelt as a running mate, and Roosevelt himself opposed the suggestion: "I will not accept under any circumstances and that is all there is about it." Platt, however, engineered a draft movement to nominate the rough-riding Colonel for the second spot. Mark Hanna, the G.O.P. national chairman, erupted: "Don't any of you realize there's only one life between this madman and the White House?" For his own part, Roosevelt said with apparent remorse: "I do not expect to go any further in politics." But he waged a colorful campaign, and his vast popularity greatly increased McKinley's margin of victory.

The Vice Presidency, with its built-in aura of "second best," depressed the mercurial Roosevelt. But his tedium was shattered on September 13, 1901. While hunting in the Adirondacks, he received word that McKinley, shot by a fanatic a week earlier, was close to death. After a heroic nighttime descent down tortuous, pitch-black mountain roads, Roosevelt arrived in Buffalo, where, on September 14, 1901, he took the oath of office as the twenty-sixth President of the United States. The man who had condemned McKinley's victory in 1896 as a triumph of America's "gold-ridden, capitalist-bestridden, usurer-mastered future" had succeeded him in the White House. "Now look," cried Hanna, "that damned cowboy is President of the United States!"

Assuring Hanna that he would go slowly, the forty-two-year-old Roosevelt announced that he would "continue, absolutely unbroken" the policies of McKinley. The youngest man ever to accede to the Presidency (although John F. Kennedy would be the youngest to be elected to it), Roosevelt wrote: "It is a dreadful thing to come into the Presidency this way; but it would be a far worse thing to be morbid about it. Here is the task, and I have got to do it to the best of my ability. . . ."

Teddy Roosevelt rose to presidential power at a moment of unprecedented social and economic ferment in the nation, which was being rocked by a surging progressive movement that demanded an end to the abuses of an incredibly heartless industrial capitalism, if not to capitalism itself. The progressive cause was espoused by Populists, labor unions, farmers, and workers who cried out for correction of foul working conditions, recurrent depressions, management coercion, and the declining value of real wages. They protested the affluent reign of a big-business aristocracy and of uncontrolled trusts. The oppressed found eloquent champions in Upton Sinclair, Ida Tarbell, Frank Norris, Lincoln Steffens, and Brand Whitlock, who wrote, in fiction and nonfiction, a classic literature of exposure and protest. Progressives such as Robert M. La Follette and William Jennings Bryan and less moderate Socialists such as Eugene V. Debs led the formal political fight for economic reform:

an eight-hour day, a graduated income tax to counter inequities, public ownership of utilities, and varying degrees of government supervision of industry.

All now looked to the popular young President to see what he would do. He did not disappoint the majority of Americans. If Roosevelt could accept "the inevitableness of combinations in business" and dismiss as "rural toryism" progressive attempts to restore the less complicated milieu of mid-nineteenth-century capitalism, he was no less aware than the progressives of the industrial abuses that threatened to precipitate revolt against the very foundations of American society. And though himself a scion of patrician wealth, Roosevelt became a major voice in the progressive movement, lending it the immense prestige of the Presidency.

The new President struck out against the "criminal rich," declaring that "of all forms of tyranny, the least attractive and the most vulgar is the tyranny of mere wealth, the tyranny of plutocracy." He was careful to couch his orations in terms of loyalty to the free enterprise system, assuring big business that his primary aim was to protect capitalism against both socialism and itself.

Roosevelt was not paying mere lip service to reform, as he proved by two decisive confrontations with big business in his first term. Barely six months after his accession to the Presidency, Roosevelt moved against the trusts—illegal combinations of big-business corporations, organized to stifle competition and control prices and rates through collusion. Acting under the neglected Sherman Antitrust Act of 1890, the President filed suit against the powerful Northern Securities Company, a holding company organized by J. Pierpont Morgan and his associates to monopolize transportation in the Northwest by merging three railroad systems. The Supreme Court had declared in 1895 that Congress had no power to prohibit a holding company's operations. But T. R. pressed the fight, filing similar suits against trusts in the beef, coal, and sugar industries. And in

T. R. and John Burroughs posed at Yellowstone Park in 1903. A lifelong outdoorsman, Roosevelt called a national conservation conference in 1908, after which many states formed their own conservation commissions.

1904 the Supreme Court concurred in a decree by the United States circuit court at St. Paul that Northern Securities should be dissolved. An angry J. P. Morgan rushed to the White House, assuring Roosevelt: "We can easily compromise the matter." The President's reply: "There can be no compromise in the enforcement of the law."

In May, 1902, T. R. faced what was perhaps the greatest challenge to his presidential leadership during his entire tenure in the White House. When the United Mine Workers called a strike of 150,000 men for better wages and working conditions, the mine owners, led by Morgan interests and typified by George F. Baer, president of the Philadelphia and Reading Railroad, refused to compromise. Said Baer: "The rights and interests of the laboring man will be protected and cared for—not by the labor agitators, but by the Christian men to whom God in his infinite wisdom has given the control of the property interests of this country." In an attempt to bring pressure on both strikers and management, as well as to win support for his trust-busting policies, Roosevelt embarked on a speaking tour that took him to the Midwest and to New England. Injuries sustained in Pittsfield, Massachusetts, where an electric trolley slammed into his carriage, ended the tour and confined the President to a wheel chair for weeks.

Concerned about the danger of a coal famine as fall approached, Roosevelt asserted the President's right and duty to protect the public interest against assaults by either labor or management. He urged both sides to accept arbitration of the strike. The mine workers agreed but management refused, charging the President with illegal interference in the affairs of business.

Despite a new burst of public anger, industry remained adamant, refusing, at a White House conference on October 3, to accept the union's demands or arbitration and declining to offer terms of its own. An enraged Roosevelt again warned of the revolutionary potential of a coal famine, predicting "the most terrible riots that this country has ever seen." Then the President acted on

his own, making plans, he later revealed, to instruct the Army to seize and operate the coal mines. "I did not intend," he said later, "to sit supinely when such a state of things was impending." Through J. P. Morgan the administration issued its ultimatum to the coal operators, who agreed to support an impartial commission's investigation of the dispute. The workers returned to the mines pending the inquiry. "The whole country breathed freer," said the President, "and felt as if a nightmare had been lifted. . . ."

It was a landmark in presidential initiative and leadership, casting Teddy Roosevelt irrevocably in the image of a popular crusader. Undeterred by the disapproval of his own class, T. R. remained convinced that he had acted correctly. ". . . The Buchanan principle of striving to find some constitutional reason for inaction" was not for him, he declared. Nor did he care for "the little, feeble, snarling men who yell about executive usurpation" whenever a President acts with strength. "My business," he wrote in 1903, "is to see fair play among all men, capitalists or wageworkers," and to face great national crises with "immediate and vigorous executive action." All he wanted, he said, was "to see to it that every man has a square deal, no more and no less."

In 1903 T. R. pursued the Square Deal in an astonishing series of domestic reforms. He established the Department of Commerce and Labor, committing it to increasing industrial growth and improving working conditions; its Bureau of Corporations, one historian wrote, was to be "the eye of the government in matters of business." The Expedition Act gave the United States power to obtain prompter trials of those being prosecuted under the interstate commerce or antitrust laws. The Elkins Act strengthened the Interstate Commerce Commission by forbidding railroads to deviate from published rate schedules. And Roosevelt personally urged states to prohibit the employment of women or children in industries afflicted by unsafe or unsanitary conditions.

In his first term Roosevelt also initiated a vigorous and farsighted program of conservation, beginning with the Reclamation Act of 1902 and the enlargement of the Bureau of Forestry. Defying the landed interests, the President moved to redeem and irrigate neglected or despoiled land in the West. A commission was named in 1903 to study national resources and recommend optimum uses of land. Interstate cooperation was encouraged at regional conferences held through federal incentive. T. R. considered conservation second only to trust-busting as "the most vital internal question of the United States." And he carried the gospel throughout the land: "I recognize the right and duty of this generation to develop and use the natural resources of our land; but I do not recognize the right to waste them, or to rob, by wasteful use, the generations that come after us." Roosevelt went well beyond rhetoric. He set aside some 150,000,000 acres of timberland for national use, established fifty game preserves, doubled the number of national parks, and founded sixteen national monuments.

In foreign policy, too, Roosevelt demonstrated extraordinary executive vigor. An unabashed expansionist, he was committed to a policy of power through naval supremacy, imperial control of the Pacific, and hemispheric dominion. America, he said, was no longer insulated by protective oceans; sea power and modern technology were dissolving old barriers. "We have no choice as to whether or not we shall play a great part in the world," he declared. ". . . All that we can decide is whether we shall play it well or ill." To play the game well, he said, a big stick— ever ready for swinging—was essential.

On December 16, 1901, Roosevelt secured Senate ratification of the second Hay-Pauncefote Treaty, which enabled the United States to emerge as a major military and commercial power. In the treaty, which abrogated earlier agreements, Britain acquiesced to the United States desire to construct a Central American canal in a neutral canal zone. On June 28, 1902, Congress authorized T. R. to build a canal across Panama (then a part of Colombia) on the condition that the President could buy rights from

the New Panama Canal Company, the French group that had failed in its attempt to build a canal, and acquire from Colombia permanent control of a canal zone.

The Hay-Hernan Convention, signed with Colombia on January 22, 1903, met United States terms. In less than two months the United States Senate ratified the treaty, but Colombia's legislature rejected it in August, demanding more money and objecting to what it considered an assault on Colombia's sovereignty. An angry Roosevelt assured Mark Hanna that he would "warn these cat-rabbits that great though our patience has been, it can be exhausted." Conveniently, however, Panama declared its independence in a bloodless coup on November 3, 1903, after an uprising spearheaded by Philippe Bunau-Varilla, former chief engineer of the French canal company, and an American attorney named William Cromwell, both of whom would gain financially from the sale of rights to the United States. Troops dispatched by Colombia to quell the revolt were bribed either to join it or to ignore it while the United States Navy stood by at the Isthmus of Panama. Within three days, the United States had recognized the infant republic and on November 18 negotiated— with Bunau-Varilla—a treaty whereby the United States acquired a canal zone ten miles wide and paid forty million dollars directly to the French canal company. Only ten million dollars and a two-hundred-and-fifty-thousand-dollar annuity were paid to Panama. The United States guaranteed the neutrality of the Canal in return for the right to fortify it.

It was an arrogant, flagrantly illegal display of American power and pressure that would plague Washington's relations with Latin America for decades. (President Wilson would urge America to offer a formal apology to Colombia, and financial restitution would one day be made.) But Roosevelt was triumphant. When Congress delayed its decision on the Canal, Roosevelt boasted: "I took the Canal Zone, and let Congress debate, and while the debate goes on, the canal does so also." International propriety aside, there could be no question of the Canal's immense strategic and commercial importance. It made America a major Pacific sea power, a check, as Roosevelt intended, on Japanese and Russian expansion.

As Chief Executive, T. R. also sustained the United States hegemony in Central and South America. When Great Britain, Germany, and Italy blockaded Venezuelan ports in 1902, insisting that Venezuela pay its debts, Roosevelt dispatched Dewey's fleet to Caribbean waters, warning Kaiser Wilhelm II that invasion would be met with naval force. The dispute was submitted to arbitration, and the blockade was lifted in 1903. Similarly, when European powers sought to compel the Dominican Republic to pay its debts in 1904, T. R. proclaimed the celebrated Roosevelt Corollary to the Monroe Doctrine. Continued foreign intervention or wrongdoing in the Western Hemisphere, Roosevelt warned, might force the United States, "however reluctantly . . . to the exercise of an international police power" to repel invaders. T. R. did not content himself with preaching. He persuaded the Dominican Republic to establish a financial receivership whereby an American comptroller would collect and disburse its revenues. Without waiting for congressional approval, Roosevelt dispatched his comptroller to the Caribbean nation. "I put the agreement into effect . . ." Roosevelt declared, "and I would have continued it until the end of my term, if necessary, without any action by Congress."

In another important success T. R. secured Britain's support in settling with Canada the thorny issue of the Alaskan boundary. In 1903 a commission of three Americans, two Canadians, and one Briton voted in favor of the United States, providing new cement for the emerging Anglo-American entente.

Roosevelt's concept of the Presidency was no less explicit in words than in deeds. A prolific writer, he unequivocally expressed his belief in a strong Presidency. "I believe," he wrote in 1908, "that the efficiency of this Government depends upon its possessing a strong central executive, and wherever I

At twenty, "Princess" Alice Roosevelt had begun a lifetime of participation in Capital social life.

could establish a precedent for strength in the executive . . . I have felt . . . [that] I was establishing a precedent of value." The President's power, he argued, is "limited only by specific restrictions and prohibitions appearing in the Constitution or imposed by the Congress under its Constitutional powers."

The White House during the Roosevelt years rang with the joy of life: Alice Roosevelt, with her runabout and cigarettes, embodiment of the Emancipated Woman; the irrepressible Theodore, Jr., Kermit, Ethel, Archie, and Quentin, romping with a bear named Jonathan Edwards and a guinea pig named Father Grady (after a family friend), or sneaking the family pony into the White House to comfort an ailing sibling. Edith Roosevelt, handsome and statuesque, brought a new, more natural dignity to the White House; an archetypal First Lady, she was entirely at ease with elegance.

But it was T. R. himself, contagiously energetic, who held the White House spotlight. "I enjoy being President," he said in 1903, and America shared his joy through its

669

Sunday newspapers. Roosevelt made the Presidency come alive. He "belonged" to the people, representing at once what they were and what they wanted. The man on the street could identify with him: pillow fighting with his children after critical sessions of state, sparring with John L. Sullivan in the White House gym, getting away from it all to hunt panthers in Colorado. He was perennially young. Quipped one observer: "You must always remember that the President is about six."

Roosevelt was always at the center of action, and by design. "When Theodore attends a wedding," a relative sighed, "he wants to be the bride, and when he attends a funeral he wants to be the corpse." Critics found him pushy, but as novelist Owen Wister wrote, "A creature charged with such a voltage as his, became the central presence at once, whether he stepped on a platform or entered a room." T. R. read Tacitus and Milton or played tennis and medicine ball in free moments. In one White House jujitsu session, he had the pleasure of seeing Secretary of War William Howard Taft's three-hundred-pound hulk expertly floored by a diminutive Japanese.

The hero of American youth, Roosevelt arose at 6 A.M. for push-ups and boxed daily. He championed the fifty-mile hike, rode to hounds, and played football on the White House lawn. When he was not exercising or running the government, he headed a Boy Scout troop in Oyster Bay, Long Island, or wrote books, such as *Winning the West*.

Teddy Roosevelt was a President of "firsts." He was the first President to leave the shores of the United States while in office—in a 1908 visit to the Panama Canal site. He was the first Republican President from the East and the first Vice President who acceded to the Presidency to be elected to the office in his own right. He was the first President to fly (though not until 1910), and the purchase of a twenty-five-thousand-dollar plane from the Wright brothers during his Presidency gave birth to the U.S. Army Air Forces. He was the first President to invite a Negro—Booker T. Washington—

to dine at the White House. He established a White House press room, added two office wings to the Mansion to ensure greater family privacy, and originated such classic American expressions as "lunatic fringe" and "my hat is in the ring." An act of mercy while hunting—T. R.'s refusal to shoot a small bear—inspired a cherished American toy, the Teddy bear.

No tight-lipped conformity or discreet silence for T. R. He loved hard and hated hard and never hesitated to declare an opinion on any subject that caught his attention. To disagree with him, in his mind, was tantamount to moral subversion. "He killed mosquitoes," writes one biographer, "as if they were lions." T. R.'s anger, his valet recalled, "was a thing to behold. But it was extremely rare." It must often have been as transparent as it was rare, for many of his adversaries forgave T. R.'s bluster. As Irvin Cobb put it: "You had to hate the Colonel a whole lot to keep from loving him."

As his first term ended, Roosevelt could not look forward to the Republican nomination with unqualified certainty, for he had alienated large segments of the Republican party and many big-business men. But the election of 1904 was to prove that he could still muster the support of some of the nation's biggest money men. Aware, no doubt, of T. R.'s formidable value as a safety valve of reform, Morgan, Harriman, Rockefeller, Frick, and Gould cheerfully backed him. Running against the colorless Alton B. Parker, the Colonel galloped to victory, 7,628,461 votes to 5,084,223.

Escorted to the Capitol steps by cowboys, Indians, and the inevitable Rough Riders on March 4, 1905, Roosevelt delivered an Inaugural Address notable for its brevity and for its consciousness of America's new role in the world. "We have become a great nation, forced by the fact of its greatness into relations with the other nations of the earth, and we must behave as beseems a people with such responsibilities." Wearing a ring containing a lock of hair from Lincoln's brow, the President continued: "Our forefathers faced certain perils which we have

DRAWING THE LINE IN MISSISSIPPI

Copyright, 1906, by Edward Stern & Co., Inc.

"They spent some days in seeing the town:
Doing Fifth Avenue up and down."

T. R.'s refusal to shoot a bear cub became an instant legend, first inspiring cartoons and then a series of stories, The Adventures of the Roosevelt Bears. *Above right, the Teddy bears stroll down Fifth Avenue.*

outgrown. We now face other perils, the very existence of which it was impossible that they should foresee." The development of corporate capitalism, T. R. declared, had given America "marvelous material well-being," but had also imposed "the care and anxiety inseparable from the accumulation of great wealth in industrial centers." This crisis, Roosevelt warned, must be faced squarely and solved: "If we fail, the cause of free self-government throughout the world will rock to its foundations. . . ."

Now President in his own right, Theodore Roosevelt resumed his battle against the abuses of big business. In 1906 he signed the Pure Food and Drug Act, prohibiting the manufacture, sale, or interstate transportation of adulterated food, drugs, medicine, or liquor, and requiring honest labeling of ingredients. An act was passed ordering the regular inspection of stockyards and packing houses. The Hepburn Act gave the Interstate Commerce Commission the right to regulate the rates of railroads, express companies, and terminal facilities.

Roosevelt has been accused of using reform largely as an instrument of political power. It is pointed out that even in the famed Northern Securities case no criminal prosecutions were pursued. It is noted that the more conservative Taft instituted almost twice as many suits against the trusts as did T. R. It has been shown that despite his image as a popular crusader, T. R.'s major advisers were industrialists or bankers. It is lamented that in seizing leadership of the progressive movement from men such as La Follette and Bryan, Roosevelt in fact emasculated it. Even on the purely human level of race relations, it is argued, T. R.'s agreement with Booker T. Washington to appoint "just enough [Negroes] to make it evident that they were not being entirely proscribed" embodied unconscionable hypocrisy.

These criticisms cannot be denied. Roosevelt was unquestionably a pragmatic politician, a realist unwilling to risk personal position for pie in the sky. He worked with his party as closely as possible. "One must learn . . ." he said, "not to jeopardize one's power for doing the good that is possible by efforts to correct evils over which one has no control. . . ." Roosevelt was not a basic theorist, as Jefferson had been. He did not seek a fundamental change in the socio-economic structure. Embodying and sustaining the central prejudices and interests of his class, he was concerned less with the sources than with the unsettling symptoms

ALTON B. PARKER

Teddy Roosevelt, fast becoming a popular legend in his own time, was opposed in 1904 by honest, straightforward, colorless Judge Alton B. Parker. Appealing to big business, the Democrats portrayed Parker as a staunch conservative; but as one newspaper said, industry preferred "the impulsive candidate of the party of conservatism to the conservative candidate of the party which business interests regard as permanently and dangerously impulsive." Parker was defeated, as one wag put it, "by acclamation." Had the Democrats given a truer picture of their candidate, the landslide might not have been so severe. Born and educated in upstate New York, Parker had been elected Ulster County surrogate in 1877. At every subsequent point in his judicial rise he showed himself to be a leading Democratic vote getter and a loyal supporter of his party's candidates. By 1897 he had been named chief justice of the state court of appeals. Parker's judicial record was generally liberal—decidedly so in labor cases. He did nothing to promote his own candidacy in 1904, fearing that he might discredit himself as a judge, and insisted on informing the convention that he advocated the gold standard. Nevertheless, he was nominated on the first ballot. But the handwriting was on the wall, and William Jennings Bryan, the nominee in the two previous elections, remarked, "As soon as the election is over I shall . . . organize for the campaign of 1908."

of social evil. Where radicals would sew a new fabric, he patched. But when all this is said, it remains incontestable that Roosevelt wrote a record of reform without precedent in America. He gave voice and dignity to the great cry for justice that Americans too long had dared not speak.

Always he stressed executive leadership and federal priority. Roosevelt personally coerced, for example, the San Francisco school authorities to act reasonably when that city's exclusion and segregation of Japanese school children critically strained relations between Washington and Tokyo. Through Roosevelt's efforts Japan agreed to sign the famed "Gentleman's Agreement" of 1908, which restricted the emigration of Japanese labor to the United States.

In foreign affairs T. R.'s second term was no less dramatic than the first. Alarmed by Japan's victories over Russia at Port Arthur and Mukden, T. R. personally prevailed on the Mikado and the Czar in 1905 to accept international arbitration of their lengthy war. Roosevelt's suggested terms of settlement were largely incorporated in the Russo-Japanese agreement signed aboard the presidential yacht, *Mayflower*, at Portsmouth, New Hampshire, on September 5. For his efforts Roosevelt won the Nobel Peace Prize.

President Roosevelt, at the request of the Kaiser, also persuaded France to attend a thirteen-nation peace conference in Algeciras in January, 1906, to settle its differences over territorial control of, and commercial access to, North Africa. In the Far East in 1908 the United States signed an Open Door pact with Japan—the Root-Takahira Agreement—guaranteeing the two countries "equal opportunity for commerce and industry" in China.

T. R. sustained his close vigil in Latin-American affairs. When an anarchic Cuba requested American aid in restoring order in 1906, Roosevelt intervened directly, dispatching Secretary of War William Howard Taft to head an occupation administration until an election could be held. Again T. R. had acted without consulting Capitol Hill.

"I should not dream of asking the permission of Congress . . ." he told Taft. "You know as well as I do that it is for the enormous interest of this government to strengthen and give independence to the executive in dealing with foreign powers. . . . Therefore the important thing to do is for a President who is willing to accept responsibility to establish precedents which successors may follow. . . ."

Easily the most decisive of Roosevelt's foreign policy moves in his second term was his dispatching of the Battle Fleet of the United States Navy—sixteen battleships and twelve thousand men—on a world cruise from late 1907 to February of 1909. The first ports of call were in Japan. Alarmed by reports of a Japanese military build-up aimed at the United States and concerned, said biographer James Bishop, lest the Japanese believe he had protected their interests in San Francisco out of fear, T. R. saw the fleet off on a "courtesy" cruise, which, he insisted, would have a "pacific effect." Japan greeted this first visit of a Western battle fleet to its home waters with enthusiasm and interest. As for Roosevelt, he hailed the cruise as "the most important service that I rendered to peace." In sending the fleet he had acted alone, as with Cuba. When the chairman of the Senate Committee on Naval Affairs had told T. R. that the fleet could not go because Congress would not vote the money, Roosevelt tartly replied that he had enough money to get the fleet to the Pacific. If Congress refused to finance its return, the fleet would have to stay there.

For critics of his interventionist and preparedness policies T. R. had few words. "This people of ours," he explained in 1908, "simply does not understand how things are outside our boundaries." Roosevelt thought he did. In any case, wrote biographer Hermann Hagedorn, T. R. "found the government of the United States in the position among world powers of a new boy in school; he left it firmly established in the first rank."

At home Roosevelt waged evangelical war on "the timid good," the pacifists, the effete. The White House, he decided, was a "bully

CHARLES W. FAIRBANKS

Although their political views were not compatible, Charles Warren Fairbanks was selected as Theodore Roosevelt's running mate in 1904 to balance the Republican ticket. Born in a one-room log farmhouse in Ohio, Fairbanks moved to Indianapolis in the 1870's and became a markedly successful attorney for railroad companies. He rose to national prominence as keynote speaker at the Republican convention of 1896. The following year Fairbanks was elected to the United States Senate, where he was an influential spokesman for the McKinley administration. The cool, conservative legislator, who controlled the Indiana Republican machine, had presidential aspirations, and during the 1904 campaign he traveled more than twenty-five thousand miles, hoping that the party leaders and voters would nominate him four years later. But President Roosevelt, fearing with good reason that Fairbanks would try to thwart his Square Deal programs, largely ignored his Vice President in public and made fun of him in private. He openly discussed his potential successors in Fairbanks' presence. Fairbanks was chairman of the Platform Committee at the 1912 Republican convention and predictably preferred William Howard Taft rather than former President Roosevelt. An unsuccessful favorite-son candidate for the Republican presidential nomination four years later, Fairbanks died in 1918 at the age of sixty-six.

pulpit" from which to preach "the fundamental fight for morality." "Keep your eyes on the stars, but . . . your feet on the ground." Be like the soldier and hunter; help restore "the fighting edge" to American life.

Teddy Roosevelt left his pulpit on March 4, 1909. On the night of his election victory in 1904 he had renounced a third term. So, having helped elect Taft as his successor, he stepped down, no longer forced, he said, to "one long experiment of checking [his] impulses with an iron hand."

Nineteen days after leaving the White House, he was off on a Smithsonian-sponsored hunting expedition to Africa, where he bagged more than five hundred animals and birds. He emerged from the jungle to review the Kaiser's troops, lecture at Oxford and the Sorbonne, represent Taft at the funeral of Edward VII, and deliver a Nobel Peace Prize speech. "I felt that if I met another king I should bite him," Teddy said.

Greeted on his return by a Fifth Avenue parade unequaled until Charles A. Lindbergh's reception in 1927, Roosevelt retired to his beloved Sagamore Hill in Oyster Bay, New York, but not for long. Angered by William Taft's decision to be his own boss in the Presidency and itching for his old power, T. R. took to the hustings. On August 31, 1910, at Osawatomie, Kansas, he delivered the most radical speech of his life. By the Square Deal, he now said, "I mean not merely that I stand for fair play under the present rules of the game, but that I stand for having those rules changed so as to work for a more substantial equality of opportunity and of reward for equally good service." He had moved far to the left. To the anger of businessmen, he now insisted that "property shall be the servant and not the master. . . . The citizens of the United States must effectively control the mighty commercial forces which they have themselves called into being." He advocated the adoption of an inheritance tax, health insurance, and direct primaries, and called for more powerful labor unions subject to a more centralized federal government.

For the moment he had one obvious purpose: to destroy the ungrateful Taft. "My hat is in the ring," the Colonel declared, "the fight is on, and I am stripped to the buff." He raised his banner: "We stand at Armageddon, and we battle for the Lord." But the Republican convention of 1912 chose Taft, and T. R. bolted the party. Pronouncing himself fit as a bull moose, he accepted the presidential nomination of the Progressive party. Shot by a would-be assassin in Milwaukee on October 14, 1912, Roosevelt was saved only by a metal spectacle case and a folded speech in a breast pocket that covered his heart. Despite pain, he continued his speech, heroically delivering a fifty-minute address. It was a noble moment in a most vindictive campaign. Roosevelt was to beat Taft by 631,851 votes, but in the process he would split the Republican party and give the Presidency to Wilson.

After winning a lawsuit against an editor who had charged him with tippling, T. R. was off in 1914 for a crisis-filled expedition to an unknown tributary of the Amazon. He returned home with an injured thigh and gravely weakened by jungle fever. Still restless for action when war struck Europe, he urged Wilson to let him raise a regiment to fight the Kaiser. Denied this role by the President because of his age and "intolerance of discipline," T. R. raged against Wilson. In an awful act of personal vengeance he collaborated with Henry Cabot Lodge to destroy Wilson's League of Nations.

Roosevelt stumped vigorously in Liberty Bond drives to finance the war. But his spirit, darkened by his son Quentin's death behind German lines in July, 1918, was sinking daily. On Armistice Day, November 11, 1918, the Colonel, just past sixty, entered the hospital with inflammatory rheumatism. On January 6, 1919, while Republicans talked of his fitness for the Presidency in 1920, he died of a coronary occlusion.

"He wanted to put an end to all evil in the world between sunrise and sunset," Benjamin Harrison had said of T. R. In the daylight given to him, most would agree, the Colonel had not fared badly in this fight.

—WILSON SULLIVAN

Theodore Roosevelt

A PICTURE PORTFOLIO

The Toby above is just one indicator of the wide-spread popularity T. R. enjoyed. Holding a gun and a book, he wears his Rough Rider uniform.

Moving clockwise from the photograph above, one can mark T. R.'s progress—mental and physical—from an apprehensive, thoughtful lad of five to a determined-looking young man ten years later and finally to a glowering collegiate boxer, in battle array. T. R. hoped to win the Harvard lightweight championship, but never did.

A FAST PACE

I rose like a rocket," recalled Roosevelt of his early years in the New York assembly. Friends of the socialite-reformer predicted that his political career would be brief, but admirers noted that he had "the distinction of having convictions and living up to them." When his wife died, T. R. fled to the Badlands, where he ranched and wrote, proclaiming himself "a literary feller, not a politician, nowadays." But soon his vitality reasserted itself. "Black care rarely sits behind the rider whose pace is fast enough," he remarked. Back home, he campaigned for Republican presidential candidate James G. Blaine in 1884; politics, Roosevelt discovered, could provide an even faster pace than ranching.

BROWN BROTHERS

AMERICAN MUSEUM OF NATURAL HISTORY

Roosevelt headed the New York delegation to the Republican National Convention in 1884, when the photograph at left was taken. The next year he posed (above) for a shot to promote his Hunting Trips of a Ranchman. *The cowboy outfit was authentic, but the picture was taken in a New York studio.*

In the cartoon above, T. R. is being readied to fight for the New York mayoralty in 1886—a contest he knew would be "perfectly hopeless." Soon afterward he followed Edith Carow to London and married her there.

"I AM FIGHTING
VILE CRIME"

The decade beginning in 1886 was one of the most active in Teddy Roosevelt's life. That fall he was beaten in a mayoralty contest about the outcome of which he had had no false hopes. He rewed despite Victorian misgivings ("I have no constancy! I have no constancy!"); the next September his gentle Edith presented him with Theodore Roosevelt, Jr., of whom the proud father boasted, "He exercises more vigorously than anyone I know." But time began to hang heavy at Sagamore Hill; Roosevelt needed a new outlet for his energy. Senator Henry Cabot Lodge, who more than once would help T. R. along his way, prodded President Benjamin Harrison into giving the New Yorker a thirty-five-hundred-dollar-a-year post on the Civil Service Commission. Soon Teddy initiated an across-the-board program of enforcement of the Civil Service Law, and one of his first targets was Postmaster General John Wanamaker, master spoilsman. He accused Wanamaker of "slanderous falsehoods . . . sly in-

tolerance, cruelty, and meanness that would be shocking to a barbarian." Republican politicos soon were screaming for Roosevelt's head, but the public was on his side and so was the responsible press. Even the New York *Sun*, champion of the spoils system, commented, "Poor Harrison! If he has erred he has been punished. The irrepressible, belligerent, and enthusiastic Roosevelt has made him suffer and has more suffering in store for him." But Roosevelt became restive and began looking for other dragons to slay. Returning to New York to try to straighten out its corrupt police force, Roosevelt's zeal was unbounded. "I am fighting vile crime and hideous vice," trumpeted the new commissioner. And he got results. Police misconduct trials were opened to the public and press, and blackmailing by policemen was sharply curbed. Yet Commissioner Roosevelt was sure he had "offended so many powerful interests and so many powerful politicians that no political preferment in future will be possible for me."

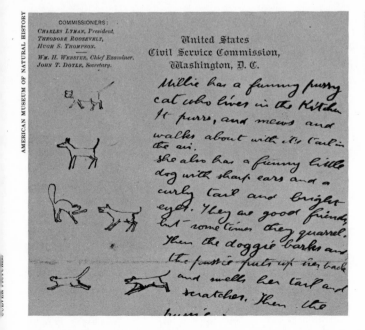

From Washington, Civil Service Commissioner Roosevelt wrote to son Ted, left, doodling some pictures in the margins. The cartoon above, whose caption begins, "He's all right when you know him . . ." reflects the animosity generated by Roosevelt's enforcement of the ban on Sunday drinking.

Before he left the Navy Department in favor of active combat, Roosevelt sent a message to Brooks Brothers, right, asking for a suitable uniform. (Brooks met its deadline.) Roosevelt and his Rough Riders chafed at having to drill—at San Antonio, Texas—and wait —at Tampa, Florida—but finally they were crammed aboard a transport bound for Cuba and glory. On July 1, T. R.'s men were in the vanguard at the storming of San Juan Hill (below), at whose summit Roosevelt found trenches "filled" with corpses of Spaniards.

Navy Department,

Washington, D. C. April 30,1898 /89

Brooks Brothers,
    Twenty-second St.& Broadway, New York.
    Can you make me so I shall have it here by next Saturday a blue cravennet regular lieutenant-colonel's uniform without yellow on collar, and with leggings? If so make it.

Theodore Roosevelt

Charge Mr Roosevelt

"DASH AND DARING"

Senator Lodge promised President McKinley that Roosevelt would behave himself if named assistant secretary of the Navy. But after he was appointed, T. R. promptly told the Naval War College, "No triumph of peace is quite so great as the supreme triumphs of war." Long an advocate of a powerful fleet, he was in favor of building new ships of all types and advised Navy Secretary Long that torpedo-boat officers should operate their craft with "dash and daring" and that the boats should be "habitually used under circumstances which imply the risk of an accident." T. R. yearned to match his actions to his words. "Destiny assisted Roosevelt in certain instances," said author Julian Street, "but he himself usually assisted Destiny to assist him." Soon he and his Rough Riders—"the society page, financial column, and Wild West Show all wrapped up in one"—were giving Destiny a great big boost.

Charles Johnson Post, painter of both the pictures on these pages, shows Teddy Roosevelt, above, in a rumpled uniform—and in one of his favorite roles.

"Roosevelt's Idea of Reorganization," above, shows the governor keeping things stirred up, as always. McKinley and T. R. were seldom together in the 1900 campaign—except on songbooks like the one below.

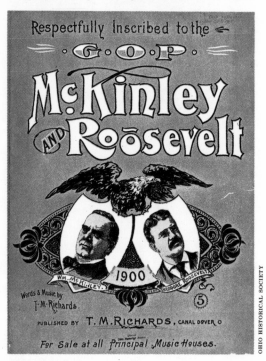

PUSHING AHEAD

How are you feeling, Colonel?" asked a reporter as T. R. returned from Cuba. "Disgracefully well!" bellowed Teddy, well aware of his soaring political stock. Much to the dismay of the reform Republicans, he soon was plotting his gubernatorial campaign with Republican boss Tom Platt. Roosevelt wanted to work within the party organization as much as possible; he told a college classmate that he planned "to be just as good . . . [a governor] as the politicians will let me be." But he could not govern without "the indispensable virtue of honesty," and in 1900 he wrote, "I have never done and shall never do one thing I ought not to do at the request of Senator Platt." Roosevelt was a monkey wrench in the New York political machine; he knew very well that Platt encouraged T. R.-for-Vice-President movements only "to get me out of the State" and was gloomy at the prospect of being "planted" for four years. When he was nominated and elected, he felt that his rise in politics was over: "I shall probably end my life as a professor in some small college." During the summer of 1901 Vice President Roosevelt divided his time between speaking engagements and taking his children and assorted cousins on long camping trips. ("My, but Uncle Ted is bully!" said a nephew. "He never asked me to wash once!") On Friday the thirteenth of September Roosevelt was looking forward to a posthike dinner at a mountain lodge when he heard that McKinley was near death. The carriage ride to the special train at North Creek was made over twisting, rain-washed roads. "Push ahead!" he urged his drivers. "If you are not afraid, I'm not. Push ahead!" The new President might have been speaking to the whole country.

The New [York]

LARGEST REPUBLICAN CIRCULATION...

VOL. XIV.—WHOLE NO. 5,036.   NEW YORK, SATURDAY MORNI[NG]...

DEATH TAKES THE[...]
AFTER A GAL[...]
A NATION[...]

Roosevelt Found by Guide When Hunting on Mountain Top, Fifty-five Miles from Any Railroad.

CANNOT REACH BUFFALO UNTIL THIS AFTERNOON

MRS. M'KINLEY KNEW OF END

Was Told Early in the Day Her Husband Must Die.

WAS BRAVE THROUGH IT ALL

Special to The Press.

ALBANY, Sept. 13.—Away on the top of Mount Marcy, attired in full hunting costume and with his gun slung over his shoulder, Theodore Roosevelt was found at 5 o'clock this evening and informed by a haggard, travel-stained guide that he was needed in Buffalo "immediately."

That word of command was sufficient to tell him what the weary messenger could not.

"Immediately," and the thoughts of the huntsman turned from the great gnarled oaks, the rippling streams, God's free air and the cool, shaded recesses where the timid hunted game sought refuge, to the sick room in Buffalo, with drawn blinds, gentle nurses, grave-faced surgeons and a stricken wife gathered about the broken form of the Executive.

FAR FROM ANY RAILROAD.

"Immediately," and he started on the long walk of ten miles to the upper Te[...]

the train for a moment in all those hours. Full steam was kept up, and the engineer and fireman remained at their posts, not even leaving the engine cab for dinner or supper, so important was this errand of life and death.

When word was sent from the lower club house that Roosevelt had passed there all took a few hours' needed sleep, as their services would not be required until to-morrow morning.

Superintendent Hammond late to-night telegraphed from North Creek that he feared Roosevelt would not reach there until 6 o'clock to-morrow morning at the earliest. That means he will be here about 8 o'clock, and cannot reach Buffalo until to-morrow afternoon.

WHERE HE HEARD FIRST NEWS.

It was on Friday afternoon, September 6, while Vice President Roosevelt was enjoying the hospitality of the Vermont Fish and Game League at Isle La Motte, near Burlington, that the news of the great national calamity first reached him. Immediately after the shooting two telegrams were sent apprising him of the tragedy that had been enacted in the Temple of Music in Buffalo, and informing him that President[...]

From a Staff Correspondent of The Press.

BUFFALO, Sept. 14.—In that unearthly light that surrounds a deathbed with all its unearthly halo a soft radiance was cast upon a woman who stood bravely by the President from the sound of the first pistol shot to the hour of gathering gloom.

It was her place, for she was his wife.

An invalid who not so long ago had been only a short distance removed from death's door; weak, and with a perfect trust that whatever Providence might have in store was for the best, yet she leaned heavily on her husband, the Chief Executive of this United States. He was not the President when the blow came early this morning she did not collapse or grow ill or cry out. She asked meekly to be permitted to see her husband—that was all. They had been together long, and could look back through it all without one faint shadow over bright memories.

ASKS TO SEE HIM.

"May I see him?" was all the wife and womanly woman asked.

"GOD'S[...]

M[...]
earth [...]

He was[...]
death in[...]
consciou[...]

The subheads on the front page of the New York Press of September 14, 1901, the day William McKinley died, focused on Vice President Roosevelt. Theodore Roosevelt was sworn in as President at Buffalo that night.

The cartoon above, "Jack and the Wall Street Giants," shows an intrepid, if tiny, Roosevelt looking for action. But T. R. did not believe in the wholesale dissolution of big-business combinations. He saw the situation in terms of "good" and "bad" trusts—and while President, saw that the bad ones ran the Supreme Court gantlet.

T. R. BARES HIS TEETH

Where are our offices," T. R. had boomed when he became New York's police commissioner. "Where is the board room? Now, what do we do?" Such bustling exuberance would hardly do as he succeeded McKinley, but Henry Adams was soon ascribing to him "the quality that medieval theology assigned to God— *he was pure act.*" Yet T. R. moved with relative circumspection. As one observer said, "He stood close to the center and bared his teeth at the conservatives of the right and the liberals of the extreme left"—and used his executive authority deftly. He hounded the "malefactors of great wealth" by putting muscle into the Sherman Antitrust Act rather than by trying to ram through new legislation; the old guard could not complain and progressives were happy.

Roosevelt was not a President who kept his "talents undamaged in a napkin." During the coal strike he justified taking action by recalling the "old common law" precept that "a peasant could take wood that was not his if necessary for the preservation of life and health in winter weather." His Attorney General had never heard of the principle, but that neither surprised nor stopped T. R., who had made it up for the emergency. Above all else was the ever-present vitality. One newspaper marveled at "the scrapes he gets into, the scrapes he gets out of—the things he attempts . . . accomplishes . . . demolishes—his appointments and his disappointments . . . his assumptions, presumptions, omnisciences, and deficiencies." Said William Allen White: "If he was a freak, God and the times needed one."

President Roosevelt poses, above, with mine workers after the settlement of the coal strike of 1902. Although the laborers' demands for better hours had not been met and the owners had been soothed with a 10 per cent hike in coal prices, Roosevelt seemed to the public to be a new and fearless champion of the working class.

Edith Roosevelt, wrote presidential aide Archie Butt, spent "seven years in the White House without making a mistake," quite a tribute to a wife and mother who had to keep a vaudevillian household on an even keel and to function as First Lady to boot. Mrs. Roosevelt's habitual poise and equanimity, mirrored in the serene painting above by Theobald Chartran, usually saw her through. Edith oversaw the remodeling of the White House from, in President Roosevelt's words, "a shabby likeness of the ground floor of the Astor House into a simple and dignified dwelling for the head of a republic."

WHITE HOUSE CIRCUS

The populace, it was said, could no more ignore Roosevelt "than a small boy can turn his head away from a circus parade followed by a steam calliope." Watching the Executive Mansion became a national pastime. The young Roosevelts, along with cousins and pals, formed "the White House Gang," roller skating in the hallways, stilt walking in the high-ceilinged rooms, roaming at will from attic to cellar—usually accompanied by a member of the family menagerie. Precocious, vivacious "Princess Alice" startled dignitaries by sliding down banisters; she carried a live garter snake in her purse; she replied to invitations with a breezy "That'll be bully!" Alice was married in the White House and cut the cake with a borrowed military saber. Roosevelt, once asked if he could not control her, said: "I can be President of the United States or I can control Alice. I cannot possibly do both." T. R., of course, was the font of all this energy, and he showed no sign of letting up. He did his best to find recruits for his rigorous "obstacle walks" (jaunts that went through, over, and under things, but never around) and truly enjoyed seeing a congressman or ambassador panting in his wake. The President continued to box, but one day he took a blow that eventually blinded his left eye—a well-kept secret. Roosevelt's friends remained as varied as his interests. White House guests included Rudyard Kipling, George Trevelyan, Bat Masterson, and John Burroughs. With a bewildered Roosevelt niece between them, T. R. and Burroughs spent a large part of one luncheon arguing whether a certain bird's call was "twee twee" or "twee twee twee." The White House under Roosevelt was a multiringed circus, and the country loved it.

T. R., Jr., and his pet parrot, Eli, posed for the photograph above in 1902. Below, would-be knight-errant Quentin and a White House policeman size each other up. The Roosevelts, wrote Allen Churchill, might have been created by Booth Tarkington.

MEN OF ACHIEVEMENT

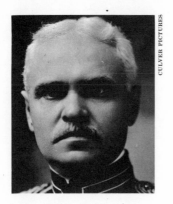

GEORGE WASHINGTON GOETHALS

"The magnitude of the work grows on me," wrote George Washington Goethals as he assumed command of the Panama Canal project in 1907. Frustrated by the resignation of two chief engineers in three years, President Roosevelt had decided "to put the Canal in charge of men who will stay on the job till I get tired of having them there. . . ." He placed the project under Army auspices and appointed Goethals, a West Point graduate and a distinguished engineer on the Army General Staff, chief engineer with full powers of administration. Virtual dictator of some forty thousand employees and their families, Goethals had to cope not only with enormous engineering problems but also with the social problems of housing, sanitation, education, law enforcement, and "a mass of irritating details," not the least of which was company morale. By taking a personal interest in employee grievances, even to the point of holding Sunday open house, he built up a crucial *esprit de corps.* When the Canal was completed in 1914, it was hailed as "the greatest engineering feat of the ages" and Goethals was acclaimed its "genius." Appointed civil governor of the Canal Zone, he remained in that post until 1916. Before his death in January, 1928, Goethals served as a consulting engineer on a number of important government projects.

LOUIS H. SULLIVAN

Louis H. Sullivan, father of the modern skyscraper, summed up his architectural philosophy in the phrase "form follows function." Born in Boston in 1856, Sullivan inherited from his Celtic father a love of grace and symmetry and at the age of thirteen decided to become an architect. After formal study at the Massachusetts Institute of Technology and the Ecole des Beaux Arts in Paris, he moved to Chicago, formed a partnership with Dankmar Adler in 1881, and became the founder of the Chicago School of architecture. His first important work, the Chicago Auditorium Building (1886–90), won international acclaim both for its acoustical perfection and for its delicate and original interior design. Employing the novel principle of steel skeleton construction, Sullivan advanced his idea of functionalism in a series of impressive designs, including the Wainwright Building in St. Louis, the Transportation Building at the 1893 World's Fair, the Gage Building and the Stock Exchange Building in Chicago, the Condict Building in New York, and many others. Stressing the vertical lines as an integral design element, he revolutionized the nature of American buildings. His *Autobiography of an Idea*, published in 1924, is a highly readable account of Sullivan's search for an indigenous style of architecture.

ORVILLE and WILBUR WRIGHT

"For some years I have been afflicted with the belief that flight is possible to man," wrote Wilbur Wright to a fellow aeronautics pioneer in 1900. Only the year before, Wilbur and his younger brother, Orville, partners in a bicycle-manufacturing firm in Dayton, Ohio, had constructed a kitelike biplane. In 1900 they built their first free-flying glider and conducted the first of their famous experiments at Kitty Hawk, North Carolina. With the pilot lying flat to reduce air resistance, the plane could be made to glide more than three hundred feet. After testing another glider with the help of a wind tunnel, the Wrights built their first powered plane, a four-cylinder machine of 750 pounds, which they launched at Kitty Hawk in 1903. The first powered flight in history lasted only twelve seconds, but it was the beginning of modern aviation. The brothers perfected their machine and two years later made a twenty-four-mile circuit flight over Huffman Field in Dayton. In 1909 the Wright brothers' patented machine was adopted by the United States Army, and in the same year the American Wright Company was organized to manufacture airplanes commercially. After Wilbur's death at forty-five in 1912, Orville Wright became president of the company; he lived on until 1948 as the elder statesman of aviation.

HENRY FORD

Even as a young boy Henry Ford had a passion for machinery. Abandoning the Michigan farm on which he was born, Ford moved to Detroit as a machine-shop apprentice at the age of sixteen, began experimenting with various types of engines, and in 1887 became chief engineer at the Edison power company. His most exciting work, however, was being done in a woodshed behind his house, where, in 1896, he completed his first motor vehicle, a crude contraption of two cylinders mounted on bicycle wheels. Five years later his more sophisticated "999" racing car broke all speed records and made him an international figure. In 1903 he organized the Ford Motor Company, and six years later the first "Model T" rolled off the assembly line. Ford had realized a lifelong dream. By perfecting the art of mass production he had revolutionized industry, bringing luxury items within reach of the average citizen. In 1914 he made headlines by instituting an unprecedented eight-hour day, by more than doubling the minimum daily wage to five dollars, and by organizing an employee profit-sharing plan. A dedicated pacifist, Ford sent a "Peace Ship" to Europe in 1915 in a valiant, if naïve, attempt to mediate World War I. Before his death at eighty-three in 1947 Ford created a museum, Greenfield Village, in Dearborn, Michigan.

MAN OF ACTION

"STAND PAT!"

The 1904 campaign button above repeats the "stand-pat" theme the Republicans had used successfully four years earlier. Roosevelt was worried about the election ("I know that after the crest is a hollow"), but his personal crest had not yet begun to break.

Now that he was in office in his own right and not "by act of God," T. R. began to press harder for reform legislation. At first he remained unwilling to alienate the conservatives and settled for less than total victory in railroad and meat-packing regulation. But soon the Senate's reactionary attitude began to chafe (he was barely able to set aside an additional seventeen million acres in federal land before a law was passed requiring congressional approval in creating future reserves). When business blamed him for the Panic of 1907, Roosevelt snapped, "If trouble comes from having the light turned on, remember that it is not really due to the light but to the misconduct which is exposed." As T. R. grew more openly liberal, he naturally fell from party grace; at the end of his term he rued that "the period of stagnation continued to rage with uninterrupted violence."

Greatly impressed by Upton Sinclair's The Jungle, *T. R. investigated the Chicago meat-packing industry, as the graphic cartoon above indicates. A law was passed calling for meat inspection at government expense, which to the progressives seemed less than the "drastic and thoroughgoing" legislation T. R. had demanded.*

Aside from the usual satisfaction he took at being at the center of things, Roosevelt must have been especially gratified in 1906 when, from the cab of a steam shovel (left), he oversaw the early progress of the Panama Canal. When Colombia had refused to ratify a canal treaty in 1903, T. R. had become firmly set against "those contemptible little creatures in Bogota" who would not give him his canal at his price. "You could no more make an agreement with the Colombian rulers," he snorted, "than you could nail currant jelly to a wall." It was much easier dealing with the new Republic of Panama—and Roosevelt got his big ditch.

Teddy's big stick went to sea in 1907 when the "White Fleet" made its "courtesy" cruise to impress world powers. Below, some American sailors try to impress the girls in Sydney, Australia.

Above, Roosevelt poses in 1909 with a testament to his prowess as a hunter. Young Kermit went along on the safari, which saw T. R. bag more than five hundred assorted birds and animals—including seventeen lions. Below, Germany's Kaiser Wilhelm II and the ex-President of America discuss world problems. T. R.'s bully European swing included "an elegant row" at the Vatican and the gift of a Teddy bear from Cambridge students.

BULL MOOSE

"All I want now is privacy," claimed Teddy, home in 1910 from adventures in Africa and Europe. "I want to close up like a native oyster." Just as he had done following his mayoralty defeat long before, he retreated to Sagamore Hill and became restless. But this time the goad to renewed activity was different. As Allen Churchill wrote, T. R. had become "a hater . . . capable of man-sized fury. . . . Theodore, who always liked to say he felt strong as a bull moose, now began to resemble a wounded one." The old Rough Rider longed to sink his spurs into the flanks of the Republican wheel horse, President William Taft. Calling his former friend "hopeless," Roosevelt ignored advice to wait and make his move in 1916. He was dead set on reasserting—immediately—the primacy he assumed he had not lost. But a Roosevelt stampede never materialized at the party convention; repudiated, he cast his lot with the Progressives. Campaigning in Milwaukee, T. R. was shot at close range by a fanatic; the bullet passed through his glasses case and a manuscript of his speech and lodged within him. Displaying incredible composure, Roosevelt put his hand to his mouth and coughed. Seeing no blood, he knew that his lung was not punctured. He addressed the man who had tried to murder him as "You poor creature!" and went on to speak for nearly an hour to an understandably astounded and hypnotized audience. Later, the examining physicians marveled at T. R.'s physique and decided it was safe to leave the bullet where it was—four inches deep in his chest. Roosevelt himself thought that he "might be stiff next morning." The election went to New Jersey's governor, Woodrow Wilson, the beneficiary of the Republican schism. Disappointed, Roosevelt successfully sued a newspaper that called him a drunkard—and then went off to explore the Amazon River.

J. DOYLE DEWITT COLLECTION

"Look up, not down—
Look out, not in—
Look forward, not backward—
And lend a hand."

Founders' Day
October 27, 1912

THE
Progressive
Party

T. R.: RU OR RU NOT? *asked a headline in the New York* American *in 1911. The following year his hat was in the ring; he felt shortchanged by the Republican convention and ran as a "Bull Moose" Progressive. A third-party ribbon appears above.*

"NOTHING TO REGRET"

We have nothing to regret," said Roosevelt after his defeat in 1912, but defeat inevitably made him something of a political outcast. He and a friend went to a meeting of the Harvard Board of Overseers and found the atmosphere icy; they were, said T. R., "like a pair of Airedale pups in a convention of tomcats." The European war, however, provided a new outlet for Roosevelt's energy. He called the sinking of the *Lusitania* "murder on the high seas" and deplored all who would put "peace above righteousness"—and that included Woodrow Wilson. The President, stormed T. R., was using "elocution as a substitute for action." When America finally went to war, Roosevelt hoped to relive old times by leading men at the front. But Wilson refused his request, "actuated," said Roosevelt, "by the basest and most contemptible political reasons." T. R.'s sons were fighting in Europe, and humorist Finley Peter Dunne told him, "The first thing you know, your four sons will put the name Roosevelt on the map." But Quentin was killed in mid-1918, and, said family friend Hermann Hagedorn, "the boy in Theodore died." T. R. suffered from rheumatism, a middle-ear infection, and a thigh wound that refused to heal, yet he still wrote editorials and articles and still read voraciously. But in the early hours of January 6, 1919, the Rough Rider died. "Death had to take him sleeping," said Vice President Thomas R. Marshall, "for if Roosevelt had been awake, there would have been a fight."

Roosevelt poses above with one of his grand-
children. He once said, "I think a baby's
hand is the most beautiful thing in the world."
On the left is Sagamore Hill's North, or
Trophy, Room, crammed with the tokens of
an energetic life. With death nearly upon
him, T. R. turned to Edith and said, "I
wonder if you will ever know how I love Sagamore Hill." The rhinoceros-foot inkwell below was kept on the former President's desk.

695

FACTS IN SUMMARY: THEODORE ROOSEVELT

CHRONOLOGY

UNITED STATES		ROOSEVELT	UNITED STATES		ROOSEVELT
	1858	Born October 27	Platt Amendment adopted by Cuba	1901	Becomes President
Civil War begins	1861		McKinley assassinated		Signs Hay-Pauncefote Treaty
Lee surrenders	1865		Philippine Government Act	1902	Enforces antitrust laws
	1880	Graduates from Harvard			Forces arbitration of anthracite coal strike
		Marries Alice Lee	U.S. recognizes Republic of Panama	1903	Directs negotiations for Panama Canal Zone
		Enrolls in law school			Settles Alaska boundary dispute
Arthur becomes President	1881	Elected to New York State assembly	U.S. intervenes in the Dominican Republic	1904	Issues corollary to Monroe Doctrine
	1884	Alice Roosevelt dies			Elected President
	1886	Runs unsuccessfully for mayor of New York		1905	Mediates Russo-Japanese peace treaty
		Marries Edith Carow	Hepburn Act	1906	Effects immigration compromise with Japan
Benjamin Harrison inaugurated	1889	Appointed U.S. civil service commissioner	Pure Food and Drug Act		
	1895	Appointed president of N.Y. Board of Police Commissioners	Financial panic	1907	Sends U.S. Navy on voyage around the world
McKinley elected President	1896		Taft elected President	1908	Calls White House Conservation Conference
	1897	Appointed assistant secretary of the Navy		1909	Ends presidential term
					Embarks on safari
Spanish-American War	1898	Organizes "Rough Riders"	Wilson elected President	1912	Runs for President on Progressive party ticket
Annexation of Hawaii				1913	Leaves for South America
Philippines, Puerto Rico, and Guam ceded to U.S.		Commands forces at Kettle Hill	Wilson re-elected	1916	
		Elected governor of New York	U.S. enters World War I	1917	Request to raise voluntary division refused
McKinley re-elected	1900	Elected Vice President		1919	Dies January 6

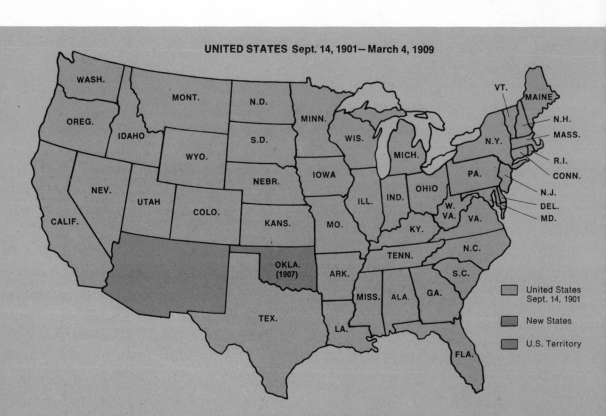

UNITED STATES Sept. 14, 1901 — March 4, 1909

☐ United States Sept. 14, 1901

☐ New States

☐ U.S. Territory

BIOGRAPHICAL FACTS

BIRTH: New York, N.Y., Oct. 27, 1858
ANCESTRY: Dutch, Scotch, English, Huguenot
FATHER: Theodore Roosevelt; b. New York, N.Y., Sept. 22, 1831; d. New York, N.Y., Feb. 9, 1878
FATHER'S OCCUPATIONS: Glass importer; merchant; banker
MOTHER: Martha Bulloch Roosevelt; b. Roswell, Ga., July 8, 1834; d. New York, N.Y., Feb. 14, 1884
BROTHER: Elliott (1860–1894)
SISTERS: Anna (1855–1931); Corinne (1861–1933)
FIRST WIFE: Alice Hathaway Lee; b. Chestnut Hill, Mass., July 29, 1861; d. New York, N.Y., Feb. 14, 1884
FIRST MARRIAGE: Brookline, Mass., Oct. 27, 1880
SECOND WIFE: Edith Kermit Carow; b. Norwich, Conn., Aug. 6, 1861; d. Oyster Bay, N.Y., Sept. 30, 1948
SECOND MARRIAGE: London, England, Dec. 2, 1886
CHILDREN: Alice Lee (1884–   ); Theodore (1887–1944); Kermit (1889–1943); Ethel Carow (1891–   ); Archibald Bulloch (1894–   ); Quentin (1897–1918)
EDUCATION: Private tutoring; B.A. from Harvard; studied law at Columbia
HOMES: 28 East 20th Street, New York, N.Y.; Sagamore Hill, Oyster Bay, N.Y.
RELIGIOUS AFFILIATION: Dutch Reformed
OCCUPATIONS BEFORE PRESIDENCY: Writer; historian; politician
MILITARY SERVICE: Lt. colonel, colonel, First U.S. Volunteer Cavalry Regiment ("Rough Riders"), 1898
PRE-PRESIDENTIAL OFFICES: New York State Assemblyman; U.S. Civil Service Commissioner; President of New York Board of Police Commissioners; Assistant Secretary of the Navy; Governor of New York; Vice President
POLITICAL PARTY: Republican; ran on Progressive ticket in 1912
AGE AT INAUGURATION: 42
OCCUPATIONS AFTER PRESIDENCY: Writer; politician
DEATH: Oyster Bay, N.Y., Jan. 6, 1919
PLACE OF BURIAL: Young's Memorial Cemetery, Oyster Bay, N.Y.

THE FIRST ADMINISTRATION

INAUGURATION: September 14, 1901; Buffalo, N.Y.
SECRETARY OF STATE: John Hay
SECRETARY OF THE TREASURY: Lyman J. Gage; Leslie M. Shaw (from Feb. 1, 1902)
SECRETARY OF WAR: Elihu Root; William H. Taft (from Feb. 1, 1904)
ATTORNEY GENERAL: Philander C. Knox; William H. Moody (from July 1, 1904)
POSTMASTER GENERAL: Charles E. Smith; Henry C. Payne (from Jan. 9, 1902); Robert J. Wynne (from Oct. 10, 1904)
SECRETARY OF THE NAVY: John D. Long; William H. Moody (from May 1, 1902); Paul Morton (from July 1, 1904)
SECRETARY OF THE INTERIOR: Ethan A. Hitchcock
SECRETARY OF AGRICULTURE: James Wilson
SECRETARY OF COMMERCE AND LABOR: George B. Cortelyou; Victor H. Metcalf (from July 1, 1904)
SUPREME COURT APPOINTMENTS: Oliver Wendell Holmes (1902); William R. Day (1903)

57th CONGRESS (March 4, 1901–March 4, 1903):
Senate: 55 Republicans; 31 Democrats; 4 Others
House: 197 Republicans; 151 Democrats; 9 Others
58th CONGRESS (March 4, 1903–March 4, 1905):
Senate: 57 Republicans; 33 Democrats
House: 208 Republicans; 178 Democrats

ELECTION OF 1904

CANDIDATES	ELECTORAL VOTE	POPULAR VOTE
Theodore Roosevelt Republican	336	7,628,461
Alton B. Parker Democratic	140	5,084,223
Eugene V. Debs Socialist	—	402,283
Silas C. Swallow Prohibition	—	258,536
Thomas E. Watson People's	—	117,183

THE SECOND ADMINISTRATION

INAUGURATION: March 4, 1905; the Capitol, Washington, D.C.
VICE PRESIDENT: Charles Warren Fairbanks
SECRETARY OF STATE: John Hay; Elihu Root (from July 19, 1905); Robert Bacon (from Jan. 27, 1909)
SECRETARY OF THE TREASURY: Leslie M. Shaw; George B. Cortelyou (from March 4, 1907)
SECRETARY OF WAR: William H. Taft; Luke E. Wright (from July 1, 1908)
ATTORNEY GENERAL: William H. Moody; Charles J. Bonaparte (from Dec. 17, 1906)
POSTMASTER GENERAL: George B. Cortelyou; George von L. Meyer (from March 4, 1907)
SECRETARY OF THE NAVY: Paul Morton; Charles J. Bonaparte (from July 1, 1905); Victor H. Metcalf (from Dec. 17, 1906); Truman H. Newberry (from Dec. 1, 1908)
SECRETARY OF THE INTERIOR: Ethan A. Hitchcock; James R. Garfield (from March 4, 1907)
SECRETARY OF AGRICULTURE: James Wilson
SECRETARY OF COMMERCE AND LABOR: Victor H. Metcalf; Oscar S. Straus (from Dec. 17, 1906)
SUPREME COURT APPOINTMENT: William H. Moody (1906)
59th CONGRESS (March 4, 1905–March 4, 1907):
Senate: 57 Republicans; 33 Democrats
House: 250 Republicans; 136 Democrats
60th CONGRESS (March 4, 1907–March 4, 1909):
Senate: 61 Republicans; 31 Democrats
House: 222 Republicans; 164 Democrats
STATE ADMITTED: Oklahoma (1907)

WILLIAM HOWARD TAFT

William Howard Taft was mightily glad when he knew for certain that he would have to leave the White House at the end of a single term. During his Presidency he had lost his closest friend; many of his programs and policies had been defeated; his wife's health had failed; and he himself, engaging in political struggles for which he had neither the taste nor the temperament, had grown fatter than ever and very weary. He had run for a second term only to keep that former closest friend, Theodore Roosevelt, from becoming President again and destroying—or so Taft felt—constitutional government. He had few illusions left about himself as President. To Dr. John Wesley Hill—who suggested after the humiliating 1912 election that Taft might be renominated in 1916—he wrote that he doubted the Republicans would turn to him again. "I have proven," he said with typical objectivity, "to be a burdensome leader and not one that aroused the multitude. . . . I am entirely content to serve in the ranks." Taft was, however, underestimating himself. He could never be a member of the rank and file: neither character nor upbringing would allow it.

Taft's father, Alphonso, had been Secretary of War and Attorney General under Grant and minister to Austria-Hungary and then to Russia under Arthur. He was a remarkable man, determined, practical, single-minded. At the start of his career he had settled on Cincinnati as the city in which he would practice law because it had "very few men . . . of much talent . . . while there is an immense amount of business." Quite as pragmatically he had chosen two wives—Fanny, who died in 1852, then Louise, William's mother—and raised, with a deep, patriarchal love, six children, the conscious beginning of a dynasty. From his sons Alphonso Taft demanded "self-denial and enthusiastic hard work," first rank in class, careers in the law, and pre-eminence wherever

Joaquin Sorolla y Bastida painted this portrait of Taft in 1909.

they went. "I am not superstitious . . ." William Taft wrote to his wife as he attended his dying father in 1891, "but I have a kind of presentiment that Father has been a kind of guardian angel to me in that his wishes for my success have been so strong and intense as to bring it [success], and that as his life ebbs away and ends I shall cease to have the luck which has followed me thus far. . . . [and that] I shall settle down to humdrum commonplace practice in Cincinnati, managing to eke out only enough to support us."

It was a remarkable prophecy, coming as it did from the man who was then Solicitor General of the United States. It was, of course, not fulfilled. Taft continued to advance until he held the highest office in the United States, the Presidency, and finally the office he had wanted most, the Chief Justiceship of the Supreme Court.

The future President was born on September 15, 1857. "He has such a large waist," his mother told a relative, "that he cannot wear any of the dresses that are made with belts." Called Willie, Will, and Big Lub, Taft went to the Sixteenth District School and then to Woodward High, where he ranked second in his graduating class. (When he had ranked fifth after one school marking period, his father had commented, "Mediocrity will not do for Will.") In 1874 he entered Yale, where he became, according to a classmate, "the most admired and respected man not only in my class but in all Yale." Once again he was second in his class.

The summer after graduation he began reading law in his father's office and that fall entered Cincinnati Law School. Soon he was supplementing his education and earning an income through a job as court reporter for the Cincinnati *Commercial*. Even before he passed the state bar examination, he became, in 1880, a Republican politician, participating in his father's unsuccessful campaign for the governorship of Ohio. Later that year he supported the successful candidate for county prosecutor and was himself appointed assistant prosecutor. In 1882 Taft was named district collector of internal revenue by President Chester A. Arthur.

Mrs. Taft apparently had found a belted dress big enough for baby Will by the time this was taken.

He kept the job for only a year; he was not trained to handle its complexities, and, moreover, he found himself in an unsettling disagreement with Arthur. The President wanted to replace, for political reasons, some men in the district office whom Taft considered his best employees. Taft would not cooperate and finally resigned to enter private law practice. But he remained active in politics, and in 1887, when Taft was thirty, he was named to a vacancy on the bench of the state superior court. He soon won election to the judgeship in his own right.

In 1890 Taft went to Washington, at the behest of President Harrison, to assume the office of solicitor general—the federal government's attorney before the Supreme Court. By then he had married Helen Herron, a Cincinnati girl whose ambition for Taft matched that of Taft's father. At the age of seventeen she had decided she would marry a man she thought would some day be President. Before Alphonso Taft died, he had begun to believe his son could be President and had told him so. Helen—"Nellie"—took up where Alphonso left off.

Congress created appeals courts in the federal districts in 1891, and Will Taft coveted an appointment to a new judgeship on the sixth circuit—Ohio, Kentucky, Michigan,

Taft excelled as a student at Woodward High and was a fair baseball player, with a strong arm.

and Tennessee. But this meant leaving Washington, and Nellie tried to talk him out of it. It would, she warned, "put an end to all the opportunities . . . of being thrown with the bigwigs." But when the appointment was offered, he took it. In the interpretation of law he found the order, traditions, and relative quiet he craved. ("I love judges," he had once said, "and I love courts. They are my ideals, that typify on earth what we shall meet hereafter in heaven under a just God.")

In his new position Taft helped strengthen the virtually unused Sherman Antitrust Act. He was the first judge to state flatly and thoroughly that laborers had a right to strike. And he also sided with labor in cases involving injuries caused by employer negligence. By his peers he was considered a good judge, even an outstanding one, and soon he was in line for a Supreme Court seat.

Then, in January, 1900, his life took an unexpected turn. President McKinley called him to Washington and asked him to head a commission being formed to govern the recently annexed Philippine Islands. The Filipinos wanted independence, and there was considerable popular sentiment in the United States for providing it quickly. But although Taft had disapproved of the annexation, he now shared McKinley's view that the Filipinos would have to be taught self-government before independence could be granted.

He hesitated over taking the assignment because he hated to leave the bench. But when McKinley promised an eventual appointment to the Supreme Court, Taft decided to accept. In mid-April, 1900, accompanied by Nellie and his three children, he sailed for the Philippines. He expected to be away less than a year. As it turned out he became the first American civil governor of the islands in July, 1901, and remained in that post until the beginning of 1904. Sympathetic toward the restless, emotional Filipinos, he brought them quickly into their government. He built up educational facilities, revolutionized the corrupt courts, improved roads and harbors, and fought to open markets for Philippine products. Because land owned by the Catholic Church and rented out to Filipino farmers had for years been a source of native irritation, Taft negotiated with the Church, and even made a trip to Rome, to acquire the land for the islanders themselves.

Taft worked incessantly despite illness and despite the heat—which he hated. The new President, Theodore Roosevelt, twice offered Taft the long-awaited appointment to the Supreme Court. But Taft felt responsible for the Filipinos' welfare, and Roosevelt was able to get him back to Washington at last only by making him Secretary of War, a post that would allow Taft to continue to oversee the Philippines.

His friendship with Theodore Roosevelt, which had begun during Taft's tenure as solicitor general, blossomed into an extraordinary relationship. Roosevelt was tense, energetic, inclined to be carried away by his enthusiasms, and very conscious of himself as "the Leader." Taft was judicious and judicial, a highly competent administrator, and as faithful a follower as Roosevelt could wish. The two men encouraged, checked, and nourished each other. Taft quickly found that his role far exceeded that of an ordinary Secretary of War: he was an adviser, a roving ambassador, even a stand-in. Once Roosevelt went off on vacation, telling the press the government was in good hands. Taft was in Washington, he said, "sitting on the lid." Taft was sent to Panama to "make the dirt fly" on the Canal. He returned to the Philippines to smooth out some difficulties there and on the way stopped in Japan to discuss the Russo-Japanese War. In 1906 he went to Cuba, then in the throes of revolution, to negotiate peace.

Roosevelt had once described the qualities needed in a governor of the Philippines as being the ones that would make a good President and Chief Justice. Taft, he had said then, was the only American who filled the bill. Now, as the President looked ahead to 1908, he offered Taft a remarkable choice. They talked about it a good deal, and one night in the White House library Roosevelt broached the subject to the Tafts again. Sitting in a chair with his eyes shut, Roosevelt intoned: "I am the seventh son of a seventh daughter and I have clairvoyant powers. I see a man weighing three hundred and fifty pounds. There is something hanging over his head. I cannot make out what it is. . . . At one time it looks like the presidency, then again it looks like the chief justiceship." "Make it the presidency," said Nellie. "Make it the chief justiceship," said Taft.

The rebus on this campaign button reads, "You and I Ted," referring to Roosevelt's support of Taft.

It was an honest desire on Taft's part. Although he was in the race for the presidential nomination by the summer of 1905, he did not really want it. "If the Chief Justice would retire," he said, "how simple everything would become." But Chief Justice Melville W. Fuller did not retire, and there were strong forces pushing Taft toward the White House. Roosevelt encouraged him. So did Nellie and the rest of the Taft clan—except his mother, who thought he would be unhappy as President. When Roosevelt, unsure of what Taft wanted, offered to appoint him to a vacant associate justiceship in 1906 and promised to raise him to presiding officer of the Supreme Court if the opportunity arose, the family fought successfully to keep the Secretary of War on the political merry-go-round.

Roosevelt, by controlling the 1908 convention, gained the nomination for his chosen successor, and by casting his charismatic aura about Taft, also won the election for him. When Taft defeated William Jennings Bryan by more than a million votes, Roosevelt capsuled his attitude toward the victory in a letter to historian George O. Trevelyan: "Taft will carry on the work substantially as I have. . . . I have the profound satisfaction of knowing that he will do all in his power to further . . . the great causes for which I have fought and that he will persevere in every one of the great governmental policies in which I most firmly believe." Commented contemporary historian Mark Sullivan: "In short, Taft will be me!"

But Taft could not be Roosevelt, and he knew it. "The chief function of the next administration," he had said, "is to complete and perfect the machinery" needed to effect Roosevelt's progressive ideas. Clearly his term would be slower paced, more legalistic, and less exciting than his predecessor's. It would be disappointing to a public used to a show in Washington and disappointing, ultimately, to Roosevelt. Taft foresaw this. As his friend left for a post-presidential hunting trip in Africa, Taft wrote a fond farewell message in which he told Roosevelt that whenever he was addressed as Mr. President

This 1909 cartoon pictures Taft as Saint Patrick, driving the evildoers out of American commerce.

he instinctively looked around to see where the President—Roosevelt—was. He said he wished he could have discussed some of his early problems as President with Roosevelt and then added: "I have no doubt that when you return you will find me very much under suspicion by our friends in the West [the progressive Republicans]. . . . I have not the prestige which you had. . . . I am not attempting quite as much as you did. . . . I have not the facility for educating the public as you had through talks with correspondents, and so I fear that a large part of the public will feel as if I had fallen away from your ideals; but you know me better and will understand that I am still working away on the same old plan. . . ."

The plan of which Taft spoke largely involved reform at home, demanded by the continuing industrial revolution. Business

was tremendously powerful and not well regulated. The exploitation of land and natural resources posed grave danger to the nation's supply of water, timber, minerals, and farm land. A growing population and migration from the farms to the industrialized cities were creating a new urban America, with attendant problems. Government, too, was growing—and needed reorganizing.

On the record, Taft did not do badly. He moved quickly to fulfill a campaign promise for a lower tariff schedule—a reform favored particularly by farmers and consumers alarmed at the rising cost of living. Big business, on the other hand, having forced tariffs upward over the past twenty years, did not want them lowered, and the President had to struggle to get even a nominally reduced tariff through Congress. Economist F. W. Taussig has commented that the Payne-Aldrich Tariff, while it contained "no downward revision of any serious consequence," nonetheless represented a turning away from protectionism. The businessmen had been checked. They were further checked by the Taft administration's enforcement of the Sherman Antitrust Act. The Roosevelt years had seen forty-four antitrust suits brought against allegedly monopolistic corporations. Taft's Attorney General, George W. Wickersham, with the President's enthusiastic support, instituted ninety such suits.

Taft also initiated a bill, which became the Mann-Elkins Act of 1910, giving the Interstate Commerce Commission jurisdiction over the communications industry and making it easier for the I.C.C. to regulate transportation rates. Another act, one of the last that Taft signed, further enhanced the I.C.C.'s powers by allowing it to base its judgments concerning increases in railroad rates on an investigation of the physical value of a railroad and its cost of operation. Taft, later labeled conservative, was thus invading the "private sector." He invaded it again by favoring the enactment of a 2 per cent tax on corporate income, which Taft believed would "give the federal government an opportunity to secure most valuable information in respect to the conduct of corporations, their actual financial condition.''

In the area of conservation, Taft was again not the innovator but the legalizer. Roosevelt had, on his own authority, taken millions of acres of land out of the public domain to protect them; Taft doubted that the President had this right and got Congress to enact a law specifically giving the Executive such power. At the end of Roosevelt's administration large sections of land in the Northwest had, by executive action, been brought under federal protection as possible water-power sites; Taft quickly rescinded the order and initiated a study by the Geological Survey to determine just which acreage should be withdrawn. A twenty-million-dollar bond issue was also authorized to provide funds for irrigation projects.

Taft's governmental reforms were impressive. By keeping a close watch on administrative spending he saved millions of dollars. He set up the Commission on Efficiency and Economy to report on the financial operations of the federal government; although no action was taken on the recommendations of the commission during Taft's term, they led to the creation of the Bureau of the Budget under Harding. The Taft-sponsored Publicity Act opened to public scrutiny the lists of campaign contributions made in races for the House of Representatives. Taft issued an Executive Order bringing eight thousand assistant postmasters into the civil service. A constitutional amendment providing for the direct election of United States senators was sent to the states for ratification. And to help finance government, Taft advocated and Congress passed another amendment, which authorized federal income taxes.

All told, it was a productive administration domestically, but there were failures in domestic policy that were politically fatal to the President. The causes lay in schisms within the Republican party. Taft felt forced, by the nature of his first Congress, to depend upon the conservatives in his party, particularly the immensely powerful House Speaker, Joseph G. ("Uncle Joe") Cannon of Illinois. This meant he had to offer the *quid pro quo* of political support, and he laid himself open

to attack by the progressives, who desperately wished to replace the old leadership. When the Payne-Aldrich Tariff was passed—after Taft had skillfully won Cannon's support on the issue—the progressives were dissatisfied; some of them claimed that the law actually increased the tariff rates. This was not true, but clearly the new tariff was only a start at reform. During a thirteen-thousand-mile tour of the nation in 1909, Taft chose the heart of progressive country—Winona, Minnesota—as the place to make the unfortunate claim that the tariff bill was "the best bill that the Republican party ever passed."

His legalistic approach to conservation also got him in trouble with the progressives. Before six months of his administration had elapsed, he was locked in combat with the conservationists, particularly with the fanatic Rooseveltian Gifford Pinchot, whom Taft had retained as chief of the Forest Service. In November, 1909, Secretary of the Interior Richard A. Ballinger was charged with corruption for allowing private acquisition of vast coal lands in Alaska. Pinchot wrote a letter to a progressive senator in which he attacked both Ballinger and Taft, who was supporting his Secretary. For this insubordination the President fired Pinchot—reluctantly, knowing it might affect his friendship with Roosevelt. To his dismay, the uproar that followed eventually forced Ballinger's resignation, though the facts indicated that he had behaved impeccably.

Because of his fight with the progressives, and because he disliked using "patronage as a club," Taft never had effective control over Congress. And when, in 1910, the Republicans lost their majority in the House, Taft had an even more difficult time getting domestic legislation passed.

Nor was his record in foreign affairs impressive. He and his Secretary of State, Philander C. Knox, extended the Open Door policy to Latin America and created "Dollar Diplomacy," which they viewed as a logical extension of the Open Door demands for fair treatment in foreign trade. In the future, their policy implied, the American government's prestige—and its troops, if necessary —would be used to further American business interests abroad, while those interests themselves would be used to influence foreign governments. Because of this policy, which the United States chose to continue after Taft's term, America earned the lasting distrust of revolutionaries around the world.

Taft caused an uproar in foreign capitals when he stated that since the United States had built the Panama Canal, American shipping should be exempt from tolls when it opened. There was some justification for this point of view, but it was in conflict with the Hay-Pauncefote Treaty, in which the United States had agreed that all nations would be charged equal tolls. Taft was adamant, but Wilson later reversed the ruling.

Taft fought hard for a reciprocity treaty with Canada to lower the tariff barriers between the two nations. In July, 1911, he finally forced the treaty through Congress. But Canadians had become alarmed at the possibility that the treaty would be used by the United States as a wedge for the ultimate annexation of Canada, and in a Canadian election, reciprocity lost.

The administration did have some small diplomatic successes, but the balance sheet clearly had more debits than credits, particularly after the Senate defeated the measure Taft had hoped would be a bright achievement in foreign policy. Taft favored the creation of some system by which the nations of the world would be able to adjudicate disagreements that might lead to war. In 1910 he began sounding out other countries on the subject, but few were interested. The next year, however, treaties were worked out with Great Britain and France; the United States and each "partner" nation agreed to submit disputes to an authority, such as the International Court at The Hague. These treaties went further than earlier agreements in that they included, as potentially subject to arbitration, questions of national honor—in Taft's words, "the questions which . . . are likely to lead to war." Since there might be some doubt as to whether an issue was properly justiciable by the arbitration

JAMES S. SHERMAN

The delegates to the 1908 Republican convention, resentful that Roosevelt had chosen their presidential candidate, named the ultraconservative representative from New York, James S. Sherman, as Taft's running mate. Born in Utica in 1855, Sherman had been a banker and businessman and a member of Congress almost without interruption since 1887. He was considered an outstanding parliamentarian. For a while he and Taft got on well together; the President even played golf with Sherman—and though Taft was a confirmed duffer, "Sunny Jim" played a worse game. Sherman offered some useful political advice to his chief. He set up a committee to investigate the Ballinger affair in such a way that proadministration findings were assured. When Taft, caught in the middle of a New York State political battle between Sherman and Roosevelt, sided first with Sherman, then with T. R., and finally blamed the fight on Sherman, the Vice President dutifully kept quiet. Taft gave Sherman no favors in return and even dropped him as a golf partner. Despite the split, Sherman was renominated in 1912—the first Vice President to be so honored since John Calhoun. Taft had more than one reason to lament this fact: Sherman died on October 30, thus weakening an already losing cause. Less than a week later, three and a half million Americans voted for the Taft-Sherman ticket, one half of which was dead.

authority, each question was first to be studied by a joint high commission, composed of three representatives of each party to the dispute. This commission would then decide whether the dispute would be arbitrated. The Senate, led by Henry Cabot Lodge, encumbered the treaties with reservations and lopped off the section concerning the high commission; instead, it gave to itself and to the President the right to decide whether to present a question for arbitration. "To play the game of 'Heads I win, tails you lose,'" Taft said, "is to accomplish nothing . . . toward Christian civilization." He refused to sign the Senate's product.

One of Taft's major opponents in the arbitration-treaty argument had been Theodore Roosevelt, home from his African safari unscathed, refreshed, but decidedly at loose ends. Inevitably, he re-entered the political arena, and almost as inevitably he found himself on the side of the progressives, vis-à-vis his old friend. Taft, puzzled and sorrowful, refused for many months to respond publicly to Roosevelt's assaults. But when Roosevelt took radical, "socialistic" positions on public affairs, Taft decided to fight for re-election. Even after this open split, while Roosevelt continued to make accusations— often exaggerated and sometimes utterly untrue—Taft held back from answering. His political advisers finally convinced him that he had to answer, and he did so in a speech on April 25, 1912. A reporter, looking for Taft after the address, found him sitting alone, head in hands. "Roosevelt was my closest friend," he said, and then he burst into tears.

Fight back or not, Taft was doomed. "The only question now," Chauncey M. Depew said after Taft won the Republican nomination and the Roosevelt forces decided to run the Colonel on the Progressive ticket, "is which corpse gets the most flowers." Roosevelt won 600,000 more popular votes than Taft. But Woodrow Wilson, the Democratic candidate, won the election.

"The nearer I get to the inauguration of my successor the greater the relief I feel," wrote Taft a month after the election. And so in March of 1913, at the age of fifty-five,

he happily returned to private life. The problem of what to do with his time was solved by Yale University, which offered him the Kent Chair of Constitutional Law. He said that he could not accept a chair but that a sofa of law would be fine.

But he was not to remain a private citizen for long. President Wilson named him co-chairman of the National War Labor Board during World War I. He also continued to work for the creation of a world peace organization. And then in 1921 Harding gave Taft the assignment he had wanted for decades, the Chief Justiceship of the Supreme Court. As head of the Court for nine years, he won congressional support for reforms in the federal judiciary. A conference of senior circuit court judges, headed by the Chief Justice, was set up to coordinate the federal courts. The Supreme Court, faced with an impossibly cluttered docket, was given some choice in what cases it would hear so that it could concentrate more on cases involving interpretation of the Constitution.

Taft's role as Chief Justice was thus largely that of a consolidator, not unlike the role he had tried to play as President. This is not to say that he made no contributions of importance to the interpretation of law. He wrote, for example, the majority opinion in *Myers v. United States*, a decision that asserted the President's right to remove executive appointees without the advice and consent of the Senate. He was part of a majority that denied to Congress the right to use taxes as a weapon to restrict practices it disapproved of. He helped to limit the powers of individual states in the regulation of commerce and to enlarge federal powers in the same sphere.

His weight went down. Nellie, who suffered a stroke shortly after her husband became President, had recovered. He was happy. "The truth is that in my present life I don't remember that I ever was president," he wrote in 1925. And so he lived out his life, until a heart ailment forced him to retire from the Supreme Court in February, 1930. He died a month later.

—MICHAEL HARWOOD

A PICTURE PORTFOLIO

This postal card, made for the campaign of 1908, used yarn for Taft's tie, felt for his suit, and real brass buttons.

HEIR APPARENT

When Elihu Root told President Roosevelt in 1903 that he planned to resign as Secretary of War, Roosevelt begged his friend William Howard Taft to accept the post. Taft, then governor of the Philippines, loved his job and had already turned down a Supreme Court seat to stay in the Pacific. "If only there were three of you!" Roosevelt wrote in a letter that convinced Taft to come home. "Then I would have put one of you on the Supreme Court . . . one of you in Root's place . . . and [made] one of you permanently governor of the Philippines." His enthusiasm for Taft appeared boundless. In 1901 he had said that Taft would be an ideal Chief Justice and President, and after having picked Taft to succeed him in 1908, T.R. told him, "I have always said you would be the greatest president, bar only Washington and Lincoln. . . ."

From the confines of the law court Judge Taft (shown at top in an 1887 photograph) moved into the wide arena of world affairs in 1900. During the next eight years, as governor of the Philippines and Roosevelt's Secretary of War, he traveled some 100,000 miles. Above, he visits the Philippine Islands with Alice Roosevelt in 1905.

By 1906 Taft was thought to be Roosevelt's crown prince (above). They and Elihu Root (made Secretary of State in 1905) were close friends, referring to each other by nicknames taken from The Three Musketeers. *Taft tried to convince Roosevelt that Root should be the heir apparent, but T. R. did not think Root could win.*

JOYS AND SORROWS

The Taft-Sherman ashtray above, with the names of past Republican candidates for the Presidency on its rim, is a souvenir of the 1908 campaign.

Taft predicted that the months before Election Day would be "a kind of nightmare for me," for he hated stumping. Below, he speaks from his train.

Taft's victory in 1908 was a triumph for the whole Taft clan, which had been pushing him toward the Presidency for years. Brother Charles, for instance, had allowed Will to make the most of his promotion to Secretary of War—a post that demanded much entertaining—by giving him up to $10,000 a year. Charles also reportedly spent $800,000 to propel him into the White House. Now, as Will, his wife Nellie, and their three children took over the Mansion, their administration promised to be as happy and brilliant as Taft's famous smile. The salary of the President had just been increased to $75,000 a year, with a $25,000 travel allowance. Nellie dressed the servants in livery and brought in so many Philippine-style furnishings and so many greens and flowers that the White House became known as the Malacañan Palace— the name of the Philippine governor's home. As expected, their party-giving was spectacular; and their administration was marked by a number of pleasant "firsts." Taft was the original golfer-President. He was the first to throw out the baseball to open the American League season. Nellie planted the first of many cherry trees from Japan at the Tidal Basin in Washington. Taft was the first to have an official presidential automobile, and the White House stables were replaced by a garage. For the first time a biplane landed on the south lawn. There was also a "last": after Taft, no President kept a cow. But all told, the Taft family's term in the Executive Mansion was not very pleasant. Nellie had a stroke a few months after the inaugural festivities and turned most of her duties as hostess over to her sisters and her daughter, Helen. President Taft quickly became exhausted by his responsibilities as Chief Executive and chief of the divided Republican party. He grew fatter than ever and began falling asleep in public.

Helen—Nellie—Taft (left, in 1909) wanted to be First Lady more than her husband wanted to be President. Therefore, she did not believe he should go onto the Supreme Court, no matter how deeply he desired to; before 1908 she thought the subject "cropped up with . . . annoying frequency." Handsome and strong-minded—and occasionally a bit waspish—she was an able and beloved helpmate. When she suffered a stroke soon after her husband's inauguration, William Taft painstakingly taught her to talk again.

Taft's size was a subject of national humor. Once, when he was in the Philippines and there was concern about his health, he reassured Root that he had just ridden twenty-five miles into the hills and had "stood trip well." Cabled Root: "How is the horse?" Below, White House workmen pose in a tub made for Taft when he was President.

A BATTLE LOST

As his biographer Henry F. Pringle has pointed out, Taft inevitably uttered "at least one unfortunate phrase . . . in every major campaign" he fought as President. In one of Taft's most important battles—an attempt to secure a reciprocity agreement with Canada—there were two such mistakes. He viewed reciprocity arrangements, under which the signatories lowered or canceled duties on goods traded between them, as one method of reducing the nation's high tariff schedule. Although he had defended the Payne-Aldrich Tariff Act as the best bill the Republicans had ever passed, it fell far short of what he wanted. So in 1910 he began talks with the Canadian finance minister, and by the beginning of 1911 an agreement had been drawn up eliminating or lowering almost all duties on farm products and a number on manufactured goods that crossed the border. But in Canada, among other objections, there was a lingering fear that the United States wanted to annex its neighbor. Taft declared, as the debate went on, that in their commercial relations the United States and Canada were "coming to the parting of the ways." He repeated this phrase even after Representative "Champ" Clark had stirred Canadian anger by telling the House he personally supported reciprocity as a step to annexation. Once the measure had been enacted by Congress, at some cost to Republican unity, Taft unwisely thanked the pro-annexation William Randolph Hearst for the support the Hearst papers had given. This emotionalized the issue further. When it came to the test at a national election in Canada in September of 1911 (Rudyard Kipling wrote a warning: "It is her own soul that Canada risks today"), reciprocity lost.

Taft is depicted, at right, performing the reciprocity marriage. He has made the minister's traditional request that anyone who has good reason for objecting to the ceremony speak out, and "Tariff-Protected Monopolies" are all furiously doing so.

712

ON THE HIGH COURT

JOHN MARSHALL HARLAN

"Let it be said," John Marshall Harlan once remarked, "that I am right rather than consistent." The inconsistency he showed during his thirty-four years on the Supreme Court resulted from a border-state heritage that made him a spokesman for both nation and individual. A conservative Kentuckian, he had fought for the North during the Civil War. After four years as state attorney general he joined the Radical Republican camp, and his support of Rutherford B. Hayes won him appointment to the High Court in 1877. Harlan was a vigorous dissenter. In 1895 his minority voice defended the nation's right to levy an income tax and urged broad construction of the Constitution's commerce clause. In 1883, while his peers invalidated the Civil Rights Act of 1875, Harlan used the personal inkwell of Roger Taney—author of the Dred Scott decision— to dissent. He believed in the sanctity of the police powers of the states. He could not abide legislation by the judiciary; in the Standard Oil case of 1911 he was angered when the Court decided the Sherman Antitrust Act prohibited only "unreasonable" restraints of trade. One friend remarked that Harlan, who died in 1911, slept "with one hand on the Constitution and the other on the Bible, safe and happy in a perfect faith in justice and righteousness."

MELVILLE FULLER

Melville Fuller, named Chief Justice by Grover Cleveland in 1888, remained an old-guard Democrat throughout his twenty-one-year tenure on the Supreme Court. He believed in states' rights and personal liberty, holding that Congress derived its powers from specific grants, not from any implicit national sovereignty. After the war with Spain a series of insular cases determined the status of new American colonial acquisitions. Fuller felt that the Constitution should follow the flag and vigorously dissented when the Court upheld tariffs on territorial goods to protect mainland producers. A colony, he reasoned, should not be "a disembodied shade . . ." with its commerce "absolutely subject to the will of Congress, irrespective of constitutional provisions." Fuller had moved from Maine to Chicago in 1856, when he was twenty-three. His conscientiousness and his intelligence made him a successful lawyer in cases ranging from ecclesiastical disputes to municipal contracts. An active Democrat, his anti-Blaine campaigning in 1884 won Cleveland's gratitude. Fuller was noted for the dignity, tact, and good humor with which he ran his Court. He was also a regent of the Smithsonian Institution and a trustee of his alma mater, Bowdoin College. Chief Justice Fuller died on the Fourth of July, 1910.

EDWARD D. WHITE

The man whose "rule of reason" dictum in the Standard Oil case of 1911 so galled John Harlan was Supreme Court Chief Justice Edward D. White. In his twenty-seven years on the High Court, White left a puzzling, self-contradictory record. He dissented, for instance, in *Lochner v. New York*, which invalidated a New York law setting a ten-hour day for bakers; yet he also dissented in *Bunting v. Oregon*, which upheld a similar law. He concurred in upholding a New York workmen's compensation act, but dissented in a case sustaining a similar law in Washington. A native of Louisiana, White served in the Confederate army and then entered Louisiana politics. He was a state senator and a member of the state supreme court before his election to the United States Senate in 1890. Cleveland appointed him to the Supreme Court in 1894 for political reasons, and White's elevation to Chief Justice in 1910 probably resulted from President William Howard Taft's wish to dissolve some of the Democratic solidarity of the Solid South. White ran a dignified, kindly Court; his abiding patience made him especially popular with young, inexperienced attorneys. Regrettably, his opinions often showed a certain labored wordiness and his reasoning was not always clear. Chief Justice White was seventy-five when he died in 1921.

OLIVER WENDELL HOLMES, JR.

"The life of the law . . ." wrote Oliver Wendell Holmes, Jr., "has been experience. The felt necessities . . . have had a good deal more to do than the syllogism in determining the rules by which men should be governed." A Boston Brahmin and a veteran of the Civil War, Holmes became an attorney and a legal editor whose skepticism and refusal to accept all legal precedents and principles as automatically valid characterized his opinions during fifty years on the Massachusetts and United States supreme courts. He played no favorites; with a singularly detached intelligence firmly grounded in legal philosophy and psychology, he was generally liberal and usually on the dissenting side. He shocked Roosevelt, who had appointed him to the Supreme Court in 1902, by sharply criticizing the Sherman Antitrust Act in the Northern Securities case, but later introduced the "stream of commerce" concept that greatly tightened federal control over interstate trade. He established "clear and present danger" as the sole basis for limiting freedom of speech (but then saw the Court disavow his dictum). Holmes hated verbosity: "The 'point of contact' is the formula, the place where the boy got his finger pinched; the rest of the machinery doesn't matter." Justice Holmes retired in 1932 at the age of ninety and died three years later.

The Taft-Roosevelt split had become a bitter national joke (as the 1912 cartoon at right indicates), and the public wished it mended. At a meeting in 1911 the two men sat side by side. "Once," said an onlooker, "when they whispered together and got to laughing, it so pleased the people that they all broke into cheering and applause." Archie Butt, a friend to both Taft and Roosevelt, grew so distraught over the fight that he went to Europe for a rest. He started home on the Titanic, but was drowned when it sank.

The defeated President was happy to leave office. Below, accompanied by Senators Augustus O. Bacon of Georgia (far left) and Murray Crane of Massachusetts, he rides in the 1913 inaugural parade with President-elect Wilson.

UNDER ATTACK

When it was suggested to Taft in 1910 that his old friend Roosevelt would try to get the 1912 nomination away from him, Taft responded, "Theodore wouldn't do that." But T. R. was clearly disappointed in the man he had praised so highly less than two years before. "For a year after Taft took office . . . I would not let myself think ill of anything he did," he told Henry Cabot Lodge. "I finally had to . . . admit to myself that . . . I had all along known he was wrong on points to which I had tried to deceive myself by loudly pro-claiming . . . that he was right." When Roosevelt threw his hat in the ring for 1912, he loosed a barrage of attacks on Taft which were not to cease for years. Taft was seen as a "Buchanan president" who "meant well but meant well feebly," a "first-class lieutenant but no leader." The well-meaning, feeble leader had, however, sufficient power to win renomination, despite Roosevelt's strenuous opposition. Roosevelt ran anyway, on the Progressive ticket. In the election in November, Taft finished a poor third, and Democrat Woodrow Wilson won the Presidency.

In 1921 President Warren Harding appointed Taft Chief Justice of the Supreme Court, making him the only man to serve as both President and head of the High Court. Taft, in his judicial robes above, administered the presidential oath to two Republicans, Calvin Coolidge in 1925 and Herbert Hoover in 1929. The genial Chief Justice, who died in 1930, became one of the most beloved Americans.

FACTS IN SUMMARY: WILLIAM HOWARD TAFT

CHRONOLOGY

UNITED STATES		TAFT
Dred Scott decision	1857	*Born September 15*
Lincoln inaugurated Civil War begins	1861	
Battle of Gettysburg	1863	
Lincoln assassinated by Booth	1865	
Johnson impeached Grant elected President	1868	
	1870	*Enters Woodward High School*
Grant re-elected President	1872	
Hayes inaugurated	1877	
	1878	*Graduates from Yale University*
Garfield elected President	1880	*Graduates from Cincin- nati Law School*
Arthur becomes President	1881	*Becomes assistant prosecutor of Hamilton County, Ohio*
	1882	*Appointed district collec- tor of internal revenue*
Cleveland elected President	1884	
	1886	*Marries Helen Herron*
Interstate Commerce Act	1887	*Appointed to Ohio superior court*
Benjamin Harrison inaugurated	1889	
Sherman Antitrust Act	1890	*Becomes U.S. solicitor general*
Sherman Silver- Purchase Act		
Cleveland elected President	1892	*Appointed judge of U.S. circuit court of appeals*
Repeal of Sherman Silver-Purchase Act	1893	
McKinley elected President	1896	*Becomes dean of Cin- cinnati Law School*
Spanish-American War	1898	
McKinley re-elected President	1900	*Becomes president of Philippine Commission*
Theodore Roosevelt becomes President	1901	*Appointed civil governor of the Philippines*
Department of Com- merce and Labor established	1903	
Roosevelt elected President	1904	*Appointed Secretary of War*
Hepburn Act Pure Food and Drug Act	1906	*Goes to Cuba to end revolution*
Panic of 1907	1907	
White House Conserva- tion Conference	1908	*Elected President*
Peary explores North Pole	1909	*Fights for reduced tariff rates*
Payne-Aldrich Tariff Act		*Proposes federal income tax amendment*
		Institutes "Dollar Diplomacy"

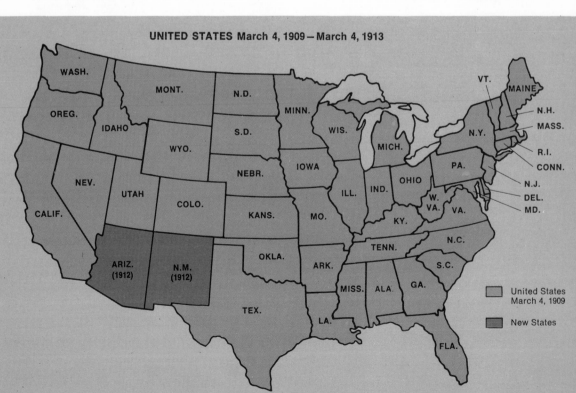

UNITED STATES March 4, 1909 — March 4, 1913

United States March 4, 1909

New States

Republican insurgents gain strength	1910	*Supports Ballinger in conservation controversy*
Mann-Elkins Act		*Appoints Commission on Efficiency and Economy*
Postal Savings Act		
Democrats win control of House		*Strengthens Interstate Commerce Commission*
		Advocates arbitration treaties with France and Great Britain
National Progressive Republican League founded	1911	*Advocates reciprocity treaty with Canada*
		Breaks American Tobacco and Standard Oil trusts
Vice President Sherman dies	1912	*Loses Roosevelt's support*
Wilson elected President		*Loses presidential election*
Sixteenth and Seventeenth amendments ratified	1913	*Becomes Kent professor of constitutional law at Yale*
Federal Reserve Act		
Panama Canal opened	1914	
Wilson re-elected	1916	
U.S. enters World War I	1917	
World War I ends	1918	*Appointed joint chairman of National War Labor Board*
Harding inaugurated as President	1921	*Appointed Chief Justice of the Supreme Court*
Coolidge becomes President	1923	
Hoover elected President	1928	*Upholds President's removal powers*
	1930	*Dies March 8*

BIOGRAPHICAL FACTS

BIRTH: Cincinnati, Ohio, Sept. 15, 1857

ANCESTRY: English; Scotch-Irish

FATHER: Alphonso Taft; b. Townshend, Vt., Nov. 5, 1810; d. San Diego, Calif., May 21, 1891

FATHER'S OCCUPATIONS: Lawyer; Secretary of War; Attorney General; diplomat

MOTHER: Louise Torrey Taft; b. Boston, Mass., Sept. 11, 1827; d. Cincinnati, Ohio, Dec. 7, 1907

BROTHERS: Henry Waters (1859–1945); Horace Dutton (1861–1943)

SISTER: Frances (1865–1950)

HALF BROTHERS: Charles Phelps (1843–1929); Peter Rawson (1845–1889)

WIFE: Helen (Nellie) Herron; b. Cincinnati, Ohio, 1861; d. Washington, D.C., 1943

MARRIAGE: Cincinnati, Ohio, June 19, 1886

CHILDREN: Robert Alphonso (1889–1953); Helen (1891–   ); Charles Phelps II (1897–1917)

EDUCATION: Woodward High School, Cincinnati, Ohio; B.A. from Yale University; Cincinnati Law School

RELIGIOUS AFFILIATION: Unitarian

OCCUPATIONS BEFORE PRESIDENCY: Lawyer; judge

PRE-PRESIDENTIAL OFFICES: Assistant Prosecuting Attorney, Hamilton County, Ohio; Ohio Superior Court Judge; U.S. Solicitor General; Federal Circuit Court Judge; Civil Governor of Philippines; Secretary of War

AGE AT INAUGURATION: 51

OCCUPATIONS AFTER PRESIDENCY: Kent professor of constitutional law, Yale University; joint chairman of National War Labor Board; Chief Justice of U.S. Supreme Court

DEATH: Washington, D.C., March 8, 1930

PLACE OF BURIAL: Arlington National Cemetery, Washington, D.C.

ELECTION OF 1908

CANDIDATES	ELECTORAL VOTE	POPULAR VOTE
William H. Taft Republican	321	7,675,320
William J. Bryan Democratic	162	6,412,294
Eugene V. Debs Socialist	—	420,793
Eugene W. Chafin Prohibition	—	253,840
Thomas L. Hisgen Independence	—	82,872

THE TAFT ADMINISTRATION

INAUGURATION: March 4, 1909; House of Representatives, Washington, D.C.

VICE PRESIDENT: James S. Sherman

SECRETARY OF STATE: Philander C. Knox

SECRETARY OF THE TREASURY: Franklin MacVeagh

SECRETARY OF WAR: Jacob M. Dickinson; Henry L. Stimson (from May 22, 1911)

ATTORNEY GENERAL: George W. Wickersham

POSTMASTER GENERAL: Frank H. Hitchcock

SECRETARY OF THE NAVY: George von L. Meyer

SECRETARY OF THE INTERIOR: Richard A. Ballinger; Walter L. Fisher (from March 7, 1911)

SECRETARY OF AGRICULTURE: James Wilson

SECRETARY OF COMMERCE AND LABOR: Charles Nagel

SUPREME COURT APPOINTMENTS: Horace H. Lurton (1910); Charles E. Hughes (1910); Willis Van Devanter (1911); Joseph R. Lamar (1911); Edward D. White, Chief Justice (1910); Mahlon Pitney (1912)

61st CONGRESS (March 4, 1909–March 4, 1911):
Senate: 61 Republicans; 32 Democrats
House: 219 Republicans; 172 Democrats

62nd CONGRESS (March 4, 1911–March 4, 1913):
Senate: 51 Republicans; 41 Democrats
House: 228 Democrats; 161 Republicans; 1 Other

STATES ADMITTED: New Mexico (1912); Arizona (1912)